Marijuana Stock Sec

An Insider's Guide for Making 100% Profits in the Legal Cannabis Market in the Next 6 Months

Written by

Stephen Satoshi

&

Everyman Investing

Financial Disclaimer:

I am not a financial advisor, this is not financial advice. This is not an investment guide nor investment advice. I am not recommending you buy any of the stocks listed here. Any form of investment or trading is liable to lose you money.

Accuracy Disclaimer:

All prices and market capitalizations are correct at the time of writing. Price and market cap information is sourced from official sources. All information in this eBook was derived from official sources where possible. Official sources meaning literature that is publicly available, provided by the company or official company website.

This ebook contains "forward-looking"statements as that term is defined in Section 27A of the Securities Act and Section 21E of the Securities Exchange Act of 1934, as amended by the Private Securities Litigation Reform Act of 1995. All statements, other than historical facts are forward-looking statements.

Forward-looking statements concern future circumstances and results and other statements that are not historical facts and are sometimes identified by the words "may," "will," "should," "potential," "intend," "expect," "endeavor," "seek," "anticipate," "estimate," "overestimate," "underestimate," "believe," "could," "project," "predict," "continue," "target" or other similar words or expressions. Forward-looking statements are based upon current plans, estimates and expectations that are subject to risks, uncertainties and assumptions. Should one or more of these risks or uncertainties materialize, or should underlying assumptions prove incorrect, actual results may vary materially from those indicated or anticipated by such forward-looking statements. The inclusion of such statements should not be regarded as a representation that such plans, estimates or expectations will be achieved

Disclosure: At the time of writing, Stephen Satoshi did not own shares of any of the stocks named.

Contents

Stock Investing for Beginners

Marijuana Stocks - 10 Penny Stocks Under $1 which Could Explode in the 2019 Pot Stock and Cannabis Business Boom

Written By

Stephen Satoshi

2019 in the Marijuana Industry so far

This has certainly been a year for marijuana "firsts." Since the year began, Cronos Group became the first pot stock to uplist from the over-the-counter exchanges to a more reputable exchange, the NASDAQ, and Vermont made history by becoming the first state to OK adult-use marijuana entirely through the legislative process.

Looking back to June, Canada became the first developed country in the world to legalize recreational marijuana, and cannabinoid-based drug developer GW Pharmaceuticals received Food and Drug Administration (FDA) approval for Epidiolex as a treatment for two rare types of childhood-onset epilepsy. This marks the first time a cannabis-derived drug has gained the FDA's favor.

In North America, according to research firm ArcView, legal marijuana sales soared 33% last year to $9.7 billion. With the expectation that compound annual sales growth will continue at an average of 28% through 2021, ArcView estimates close to $25 billion in North American sales by 2021.

Then we had arguably the biggest news of all in June of this year, after Canada became the second nation in the world (Uruguay was the first, that'll be a frequent trivia question of the next 5 years) to legalize marijuana at a federal level. The senate passed the bill 52-29, and Prime Minister Trudeau focused on the social effects of the bill more than the medical ones. In a tweet, the Prime Minister stated

"It's been too easy for our kids to get marijuana - and for criminals to reap the profits"

The bill makes it legal for adults to carry up to 30 grams of marijuana and cultivate up to four plants in their own home for personal use. In terms of the marijuana business, total spending on marijuana is projected in increase 58% in the short term. This is because most users are willing to pay a premium for legal access to the substance. The bill was obviously positive news for many of the Canadian marijuana companies which will be discussed later in this book like Canopy Growth Corp., and Aphria Inc. The laws will go into effect on October 17th, shortly after this book is published.

These statistics show that this is not just a flash in the pan industry. While marijuana stocks were originally (and somewhat fairly in my opinion) compared to cryptocurrency in terms of short term gains, there is a lot more to be said for a long term outlook here. There is medical disruption, as well as the recreational side of things, both of which are going to see a huge increase in demand as we go forward. Therefore I don't see why marijuana stocks should just be a target of millenial investors, when they can have a rightful (and fruitful) place in a retirement portfolio for example.

In terms of how specific stocks will perform going forward, I will be discussing that in depth in the stock analysis section of the book. Where I will be covering both larger companies as well as some microcap marijuana firms. I'll also be highlighting a few non-marijuana companies who are set to profit from this boom as well.

The most important upcoming date for the marijuana industry in 2018 and why this date is so crucial…

November 6th 2018 signals this year's midterm elections in the United States. In these elections, all 435 seats in the House of Representatives will be contested, as well as just over one third of the US senate seats.

This date also signifies when 14 different states will be voting on marijuana legalization of various kinds. Some will be voting for medical legalization, others for recreational.

The main reason behind this latest move is that politicians in these states have now witnessed the sheer amount of additional tax revenue that the marijuana industry can bring to their states. In most states, the post legalization tax revenue numbers have far and away outperformed expectations, which has led lawmakers in other states to get on the legal marijuana train.

In fact, in Washington State, mariuana tax revenues were $113 million *higher* than tax revenues from liquor in 2017. Colorado's marijuana industry, is now bigger than the GDP of small countries. Nevada collected $30 million in tax revenues during the first 6 months of legalisation. With figures like these being cited, it is no wonder that more and more states are now coming around to the idea of both legal medical and recreational marijuana.

It's not just a bottom line dollars and cents issue either. The Marijuana industry brings in jobs in states where it is legal. There have been nearly 1 million jobs created in legal states in the past 5 years, a number which very few other industries can even come close to. At a federal level, bringing jobs back into the country, was one of President Trump's main campaigning points, and this unexpected source of employment is a bonus at a political level. We will discuss Trump's views on marijuana in full in a later chapter.

For example, Michigan is one of the states voting on recreational legalization. The bill proposes a 10% excise tax on retail marijuana, in addition to the state's existing 6% sales tax. This would add over $100 million to the state's bottom line, and that is a conservative estimate. This then funds construction of school, roads and healthcare initiatives, making it a win-win deal for both lawmakers and the citizens of that state.

This is just one of the reasons why marijuana has gone from taboo drug to taxation golden child in the span of less than a decade, something which we haven't seen in many years. To give an early indication of what the result may be in Michigan, money donated in support of the bill is 5 times the amount of money donated in campaigns against the bill.

In total, there are 14 states who are pushing for some level of marijuana legalization.

These are

- Arizona

- Arkansas

- Connecticut

- Delaware

- Florida

- Illinois

- Maryland

- Michigan

- Minnesota

- Montana

- New Hampshire

- New Jersey

- New York

- Rhode Island

So what does this mean for the industry as a whole?

Well let's look at it this way - when California passed their marijuana legalization bill, the US marijuana market doubled in size overnight.

If states with large populations like New York and New Jersey pass their own bills, then we will likely see another doubling in the size of the market, and possibly even higher if states like Florida pass their bills as well.

And I should reiterate at this point, that for many of these states, it is a case of if, but when these bills pass. New Jersey, for example, is considered a sure thing, to the point where Governor Phil Murphy has already included $60 million in marijuana tax revenues in his next budget proposal.

Needless to say, if even half of the states listed above pass their bills, it will mean big things for the cannabis industry as a whole, and big gains for those holding marijuana stocks.

Does President Trump support legal marijuana?

In 2016, during his campaign, Donald Trump suggested that he was "100 percent" behind the idea of legalizing access to medical marijuana, and kept an open mind to the idea of recreational weed, albeit with the need for additional clinical research on its risks and benefits. But in 2017, and even within the past few months, Trump's stance on cannabis had taken a decidedly negative turn.

This has led some speculators to comment that it may be the only piece of legislation Trump ever signs that both the majority of Democrats and Republicans support. In addition to this, depending on your political views, it may be the only piece of legislation he signs that the majority of Americans support.

The bill will also provide the needed tax revenue to support infrastructure developments like the building of schools, roads, while also providing additional healthcare funds to help seniors.

In effect, Trump backed the idea of supporting the rights of states to choose what should happen with cannabis within their own borders. As you might imagine, marijuana stocks received a nice little boost after this sliver of positive Presidential news.

Of course, many pro-marijuana news services took Trump's words a little too far with takes such as.

"Marijuana industry [is] poised for supercharged growth thanks to President Trump"

"Trump announces unprecedented support for legalizing marijuana."

That's a bit far in my opinion, but it is a more positive showing from the President at least.

The biggest hurdle facing the marijuana industry today (or is it?)

Jeff Sessions has long since been the boogeyman of the marijuana industry. Attorney General Sessions anti-marijuana discourse has been stuff of legend over the past few years, and he showed his biased, and often out of touch views on the subject. He even went as far as requesting that Congress repeal the Rohrabacher-Farr Amendment, which is what protects medical marijuana businesses from federal prosecution.

However, that has all changed in the past few months. In a June statement before the Senate Science Appropriations Subcommitee, Sessions stated that *"there may well be some benefits from medical marijuana."*

He also went on to say that additional funds have been earmarked for federal cannabis research facilities. Then this was followed by further bullish statements from the Attorney General, like the one below.

"We are moving forward and we will add fairly soon, I believe, the paperwork and reviews will be completed and we will add additional suppliers of marijuana under the controlled circumstances."

Sessions also said that when it comes to controlling the substance, marijuana is not held in the same regard as cocaine, heroin, meth or fentanyl.

Although this might seem like an obvious statement, when it comes from Sessions himself, then it's a victory regardless of how anyone else would take it.

I wouldn't go out and celebrate too early though, while Republicans still control congress it will be difficult to change the marijuana laws at a federal level. However, depending on how well the Democrats do during the midterm elections on November 6, changes in that domain could be coming sooner than later.

Marijuana Stocks That Should Be On Your Radar

MariMed ($MRMD)

Price at time of writing: $2.95

What better place to start than with the top performing marijuana stock of 2018 so far. With growth of over 200% this year, MariMed has emerged as one of the top marijuana stocks on the market today. But can it's past performance be replicated in terms of future growth?

The US based firm is a multi-faceted company which covers many aspects of the marijuana industry. MariMed currently runs marijuana production facilities in five different states, while also providing consulting services to other marijuana companies. The company also owns a number of subsidiaries, which produce marijuana products from cannabis strains to cannabis infused edible products, including Kalm-Corn popcorn and Betty Eddie's fruit chews.

The company's growth depends on continued domestic expansion, it is already eyeing up development in five more states, including New Jersey, Michigan and Florida.   Michigan and Florida alone could represent more than $1 billion in annual revenue for those states, and companies with a piece of the pie will benefit greatly from their involvement.

The company's financials have strengthened over the past year. This was a knock on them for a while, but with revenue up 81%, things are starting to turn around in that area. Perhaps the most important financial metric is cash on hand, which has almost quadrupled in size over the past 6 months. The problem with a lot of marijuana stocks is one of cash flow, and MariMed fixing this part of their business makes me a lot more bullish on it going forward.

Another area we should examine when comparing it to other stocks is one of market size. Because of its focus on the US market, MariMed's "best case scenario" has a higher peak than similar companies focused on the Canadian market for example. The US market is projected to reach $22 billion in the next 5 years, roughly 3 times the size of the Canadian market.

The question is ask ourselves is this, how much of this future growth is already priced into the stock right now? We've seen extreme examples such as Tesla where future growth predictions outweigh current performance, and seemingly small bumps in the road lead to huge knocks on the share price. I still think MariMed has its merits at its current price, but just how high it could go depend largely on how the market consolidates in the next 5 years. In short, there are too many small and medium sized companies for them to all be profitable going forward. We will no doubt see mergers, takeovers and bankruptcies in the space, and it remains to be seen under which category MariMed will fall.

iAnthus Capital Holdings ($ITHUF)

Price at time of writing: $4.89

iAnthus Capital Holdings is another US based marijuana company, this time one which isn't relying on the big markets to fuel its growth going forward.

The company's general approach is to avoid the bigger markets like Colorado and California, and instead make inroads in the less competitive ones. Headquartered in New York, it is one of only 10 companies given a license to cultivate the marijuana plant in its home state. The flagship project here will be a near 40,000 square foot facility which will provide year round cultivation potential. This particular facility is projected to supply 2400 kilograms per year to the domestic market. This is just the start as the end goal for the facility is to provide over 125,000 square foot of growing space.

Another project of note is one spearheaded by a subsidiary company, Mayflower Medicinals. The company will build a 36,000 square foot growing facility in Massachusetts. Their GrowHealthy subsidiary is on track to have agreements for 15 dispensary facilities in Florida by the end of 2018, giving them an additional geographical footprint in what is considered a high potential state. The Sunshine state is currently the 4th largest in terms of medical marijuana patients. The focus on medical marijuana rather than recreational looks to be a smart play, in the short term at least. There are also plans for a Florida based growing facility as well.

The firm also acquired 2 other companies in the past year after the buyout of Citiva and GrowHealthy.

It's important to remember that this is still a very small company, with total revenues of just $3.2 million reported for Q1 2018. A net loss of $13.7 million was also reported in the financial statement. While many marijuana companies are not currently profitable, this particular one is not in the greatest shape. I can't sugarcoat it, the financial performance of this company isn't great, and that is a major area of contention going forward. The big question is whether they can withstand the big fiscal storm they are likely to face in the next 18-24 months before their new growing facilities begin to generate additional revenue for them. If they can do that, then you might be looking at a bargain at its current price.

That being said, I like the business model of competing in low competition markets, rather than trying to muscle their way into markets like California, which I feel are already oversaturated. If you can stomach the poor financials, then this one looks like a good opportunity for investors who can handle more risk in their portfolio.

Namaste Technologies ($NXTTF)

Price at time of writing: $1.48CAD

The company which has been dubbed the "Amazon of Cannabis", is aiming to become an ecommerce giant for the marijuana industry. There's nothing wrong with emulating a business model, especially one as successful as Amazon's, but it remains to be seen whether the firm can live up to the moniker. The company currently operates in over 20 different countries across 30 different websites, with various marijuana and marijuana related products available. This includes accessories like vaporizers, glassware and CBD products. The company does not own any cannabis production companies itself, instead, it partners with producers and facilitates the sale of their products.

In the words of CEO Sean Dollinger "We want [Namaste] to be your everything cannabis store." Dollinger himself is no stranger to the ecommerce space, a 20 year veteran of the market, he has founded and sold 4 successful ecommerce ventures since then.

With over 1.5 million worldwide users (for comparison Canopy Growth only has 130,000 customers) and a current market cap of around $350 million, the company posted modest (in this sector at least) revenue growth of 32% year on year, total revenues for Q2 2018 were $4.1 million. A decent gross profit margin of 21% was also reported.

The biggest news for Namaste came shortly before this book went to print, as they were awarded a license by Health Canada, for the sale of medical marijuana online. In other words, they can now act as an online pharmacy and fill prescriptions for patients over the internet, this will be the first website of its kind in Canada.

The company showed its seriousness regarding the ecommerce space after acquiring data and artificial intelligence software company Findify AB late last year. Findify's business was in tracking user behavior online in order to provide shoppers with a more streamlined and personalized user experience.

You could argue that NXTTF is the company with the biggest worldwide footprint out of all the ones mentioned in this book. While other companies are focused strictly on the Canadian and US market (for good reason), there is still huge potential across Europe and Australia. In Australia for example, Namaste has around 95% of the marijuana website traffic in the entire country. So if Australia turns to legal marijuana in the next few years, this will be another huge boost for the company.

So with all this good news, what's the downside for the "Amazon of Marijuana?" Well, like any company in an emerging market, there are growing pains. The stock price fell 18% in Q2 2018 (before their earnings report) on the back of troubles with their NamasteMD web portal and mobile platform.

This portal is vital for the company because it is what will be used in their prescription fulfilment websites, and thus a huge part of their business. As well as in the diagnosis of new patients (seriously, you will be able to book an appointment within the app on FaceTime and speak to a licensed doctor). Obviously, this is a massive hurdle for them to overcome going forward, and one people who are interested in this particular stock should monitor closely going forward. However, for an app that claims to be "as easy to use as UberEats", if they do get this right, then it could signal big things for the company and its share price going forward.

Innovative Industrial Properties ($IIPR)

Price at time of writing: $38.14

Based out of Maryland, the 2 year old company is the first Real Estate Investment Trust (REIT) in the USA to focus on the medical cannabis industry, IIPR presents an interesting opportunity for the market as we move forward.

The business model is a simple one, IIPR buys properties which are then leased to medical marijuana retailers. At this point the company's total assets are worth $83 million. The company also boasts very low debt levels, which is unusual for a REIT in a growing market. Not that this is necessarily a bad thing, it's just a more conservative structure than one would see in other boom industries.

Unlike other REITs which may boast portfolios of hundreds of properties, IIPR only owns a handful of properties at present, but each one demonstrates high yield rates of 15%+. This is partly due to the difficulty for retail companies to get traditional bank financing, and thus having to rely on firms like IIPR to be their landlords. This is something which could change dramatically if marijuana is legalized at a federal level, but as we discussed earlier in this book, that proposition is still a couple of years away at least.

Because of the risky nature of their business model (once again, cannabis is not yet legal on a federal level, which presents many challenges), this should be looked at as a high risk stock.

Investors followed this sentiment and IIPR's IPO back in 2017 resulted in a lack of traction and having to reduce the number of shares available. However, this was followed by a stronger performance this year and the stock price is currently trending upwards.

As this is a REIT, you should obviously be concerned with the dividend yield. Right now it sits at $1 per share or approximately 2.7%, which is lower than you would expect, however, this is a growth industry and much of the company's capital is reinvested back in order to spur further growth. Therefore this should be looked at as a longer term hold, rather than a short term play like some of the other stocks mentioned in this book. If things do pan out the way IIPR expects, you could be looking at a yield of 3-3.5% in the future. One more area of interest is that only 52% of the company's shares are held by institutional investors, a high number that indicates a long term bullish sentiment around the company.

As I see it, the company is overvalued at this present time. The same number of properties in its portfolio does not warrant its current share price. However, you are buying future growth for this REIT, and if they can acquire more quality properties, then you may be overpaying now for what could well be looked at as a bargain in the future. You must also remember that the company has a relative monopoly in this area, and thus they won't be facing serious competition any time soon. For those looking at adding some retail estate to their portfolio, you could do a lot worse than IIPR.

Aurora Cannabis ($ACBFF)

Price at time of writing: $8.03CAD

Another one of the larger Canadian marijuana companies, this time based out of Edmonton, Alberta. Aurora currently sells marijuana in 14 different countries across 5 continents and boasts a market cap of around $3 billion (CAD). The production capacity is currently 570,000G a year.

The company's growth thus far has been down to an aggressive acquisition strategy which has seen Aurora take over 9 different marijuana companies, including two mentioned in my first book on this subject, CanniMed and MedReleaf. The company also has investments in a number of other marijuana and marijuana related companies.

However, this growth came at a cost, Aurora has been one of the worst performing stocks this year as shares dropped over 60% at one point because of share dilution to fund acquisitions. Some analysts saw these as Aurora overextending itself and saying that it overpaid for some of the companies it had acquired. Others called Aurora's management impatient for the moves while praising the growth strategy of rival Canopy Growth.

So where does this leave Aurora today? Is it a victim of the bubble nature of Q2 2017, or is the worst over? One thing should be noted at this point in the Canopy vs. Aurora debate, the two companies are focused on different sectors of the market. Canopy is more recreational focused, whereas Aurora is more medical focused. Therefore Aurora could be a takeover target for a Big Pharma company if they are looking to hedge against the inevitable decline in the opioid industry. Aurora has the assets to make it a valuable takeover target, and any firm wanting to acquire the company whole would likely have to overpay based on the future potential of the industry as a whole.

Big news came in August when Aurora was awarded a license by Health Canada to produce softgel capsules which contain both THC and CBD. Capsules are seen as a vital growth market as they are a far higher margin marijuana product than plants or oils. Namely, because they don't require giant growth facilities in order to produce them. They are also the preferred delivery method for elderly and "professional" patients as they are far more discreet and precision dosed than a plant for example.

The more good news came when Aurora announced a partnership with Alcanna, a retailer with over 230 stores in Western Canada and Alaska. It is currently unclear just what percentage of these stores will become retail cannabis dispensaries, but it will be interesting to see going forward. Growth on the international front will likely come from Aurora's presence in Germany,

Italy and Denmark. Italy, in particular, is seen as a high potential market, and very few firms have any sort of footing there.

Aphria ($APHQF)

Price at time of writing: $10.37

The fourth largest Canadian marijuana company by market cap, Aphria is an Ontario based company which specializes in medical marijuana, both dry flowers and in cannabis oils. They have both a retail store presence as well as a telephone ordering service.

The company's growth in the near future is largely dependent on the uptake of recreational marijuana come October. Aphria has already signed agreements with ith five provinces so far - - Alberta, British Columbia, Manitoba, New Brunswick, and Quebec, to supply them with cannabis for retail stores. The company also has international operations as far afield as Malta, Brazil and even an African presence in Lesotho. Its most important international division though is in Germany, who legalized medical marijuana last year. In total, growth operations are projected to reach 225,000KG per year by early 2019.

There is also a potential opportunity in the US market. Whilst limited by its listing on the Toronto Stock Exchange, the company does have an agreement in place with Liberty Health Sciences to repurchase a position in the company if federal legalization does take place South of the border. You can't neglect to look at the potential of a market that is projected to reach $22 billion by 2022.

In terms of financials, revenue grew year on year 80% to $36.9 million CAD. This reporting comes before the legalization of recreational marijuana so one would expect this to keep growing as we move forward.

One thing to note is that Aphria is a low cost cannabis producer. This is both a positive and a negative. The positive side is that as supply catches up to demand, then being a low cost producer is easier to handle any downward price pressure. Its plants are projected to sell for roughly $8.30CAD per gram as opposed to $10CAD per gram for some of its competitors. Where this becomes a problem though is with excise tax on marijuana. Right now this is scheduled to be $1 per gram, which is a higher proportion of Aphria's bottom line due to their lower final sale price.

If we look at share price, Aphria is another stock which was probably overvalued at the beginning of the year, and as such, we saw a drop of about 40% before it bounced back slightly in the past few months. That drop was fair at the time, and quite a few other companies in the sector were in (and suffered from) the same predicament. It has since bounced back 20% and looks to be trending upwards once more at the time of writing.

Aphria is an interesting proposition in that they are a Canadian company who is more likely to be reliant on the domestic market than some of the other producers. What it comes down to is that a bet on Aphria is a bet on overall demand for recreational marijuana in Canada once legalization comes into full effect in October. If you believe demand will be high, then Aphria is a good bet.

Tilray ($TLRY)

Price at time of writing: $43.67

In July of this year, Tilray the first successful cannabis IPO on a US exchange and then became only the second Canadian marijuana stock to be listed on a major US exchange, and the first to be listed on the NASDAQ (Canopy Growth listed on the NYSE back in February). Its first trading day was one of the hottest we've seen in a while with the stock up over 31% from bell to bell.

The firm is somewhat of a trailblazer in the industry and has a number of other "firsts" under its belt. It was the first company to export medical cannabis from Canada to mainland Europe. It has also made investments into Europe as well, with a 230,000 square foot facility in Portugal one of its major assets. This Portugal operation is projected to supply much of the European market, once legislation comes around in marijuana's favor in the next few years. It also has agreements and connections with the markets in New Zealand, Chile and Cyprus

It's not just medical flowers which fuel the company's growth either. There are also edibles, beverages, capsules, vaporizer oils and other medical products among the group's offerings. These non-smoking components of the industry are the ones set for the largest growth in the coming years, as marijuana patients look for an alternative method of ingesting their cannabis.

Tilray also has retail supply agreements in place with a number of Canadian provinces, most notably Ontario, the largest province, to supply cannabis to retail stores once recreational marijuana becomes legal on October 17th. This will likely show short term growth in the company's bottom line. Longer term is dependent on just how much demand there is in the Canadian market, and if there are just too many suppliers for them all to stay profitable.

Tilray is another stock which has emerged as a potential takeover target. August rumours of UK beverage company Diageo being interested sent the stock up over 10% in a single day. Tilray is one of three companies that Diageo met with, it is believed that others are Canopy Growth and Cronos Group. Because of its position on the NASDAQ, Tilray also has potential to move into the US market, once federal legalization occurs (although not before that).

Some analysts have argued that Tilray is overvalued, and that may be true in an absolute sense. However, this is a high growth industry, with huge potential markets opening up in the next 3-5 years, and thus, some of this potential is priced into the share price. You simply cannot look at a stock like Tilray the same way you'd look at a company like Procter & Gamble for example.

The short term boom/bust cycle of Tilray means that risk adverse investors should probably steer clear of this one. However, if you can handle double digit losses in a single day (which will no doubt happen in the next few months), then it could be a solid long term play, especially if these takeover talks turn into something more concrete. Overall, you could do much worse than Tilray as an entry into the marijuana market.

GW Pharmaceuticals ($GWPH)

Price at time of writing: $143.29

One of the few non-Canadian or US based companies in this book, GW Pharmaceuticals is a British based company which is listed on the NASDAQ exchange in the US. One of the best performing companies in this list, with the share price up over 700% in the past 5 years.

In my previous book, I called GWPH a good bet based on pending approval of their Epidiolex epilepsy drug. Well in June, my prediction came was proved correct with Epidiolex became the first ever cannabis based drug to receive full FDA approval. The drug itself is CBD based (no THC) and will be used to treat two rare forms of epileptic seizures. This marks the end of one of the toughest journeys in the biotech industry and was the culmination of 20 years of work from a small firm from Southern England who had to scratch and claw for government approval for a small cannabis growing operation in their early days. For those readers who bought at the time of writing, you would have experienced comfortable 20% gains.

This distinction is important for both regulatory bodies and bottom line profitability. We have seen a surge in pure CBD products in the past few years, and many countries now allow them even if marijuana itself is banned. If you're unfamiliar with why - the short answer is that CBD is the non-psychoactive form of marijuana, so there is no physical "high" so to speak. However, CBD still possesses the calming and pain relief properties that marijuana is known for.

So where does the stock go from here? Well in the short term, GWPH is waiting for Epidiolex approval in Europe, which is expected in early 2019. Usually, European authorities follow in the FDA's footsteps so this can be looked at as a foregone conclusion. There is also another drug in development, Sativex, which aims to help treat symptoms of muscular dystrophy.

Short term forecasts have Epidiolex sales alone being worth $180 million in its first full year of US sales, with this market projected to double year on year going forward. By 2022, pure CBD products are expected to overtake marijuana based medical products for the first time ever.

The company are not without competition however, may other companies are exploring the CBD space. Tilray is one, and they are focused on developing their high CBD cannabis oil, which also aims to treat child-based epilepsy. This drug is at the phase II trial stage right now. If that also gets approval, it will no doubt eat into GWPH's market share. Zynerba Pharmaceuticals also have CBD based epilepsy treatments undergoing clinical trials at the time of writing.

In terms of investment, you should look at GWPH as a biotech company first and foremost rather than a "marijuana" one. They are not subject to the same regulations as some of the other companies mentioned in this book, and their target market is drastically different as well. Biotech is a volatile sector, especially when share price often rests on FDA approval/denial for their latest drug. I think the hardest times are over with the approval of Epidiolex and the stock will be more stable going forward. If you're looking for some next generation biotech in your portfolio, then take a close look into GWPH, because it could well fit your profile.

Zynerba Pharmaceuticals ($ZYNE)

Price at time of writing: $6.30

One of the smaller cap stocks in this section, Zynerba Pharmaceuticals is another biotech company which manufacturers cannabis based drugs for medical use.

With any biotech company, there is a different timeline to growers like Canopy or Cronos Group. Recreational marijuana is unlikely to have short term effects on price for example because ZYNE's products are strictly for the medical market.

It has two major drugs in the pipeline, ZYN001 and ZYN002. The first is a THC based patch (like nicotine patches) aimed at treating fibromyalgia and the second is a CBD based gel targeting adults with epilepsy and other seizure disorders. Currently, ZYN002 is the more advanced of the two and makes more sense in the short term as THC based products are still a lot harder to overcome regulatory bodies than CBD ones are.

ZYN002 will become a landmark drug is approval is gained because it will be the first ever drug to be used to treat fragile X syndrome. This cognitive disorder affects roughly 1 in 4000 men and 1 in 6000 women and presents a series of learning and behavior problems in sufferers. However, the past 2/3 trials haven't gone as planned, and thus there is no short term positive outlook for ZYN002. As such, the share price is down by roughly 40% over the past 6 months and just over 50% since the start of the year.

There is one big red flag with this stock: Cashflow. The company has $52 million in cash, and clinical trials are expensive. This number is down from $66 million in the middle of last year, and those numbers aren't looking like they are going to reverse any time soon. Therefore it will need to raise cash within 12 months to have any chance of moving forward. Whether this is via offering additional shares, taking a loan or working out a partnership remains to be seen. But any of these methods will likely result in rough times for the share price in the short term.

A number of institutional investors have been taking small positions in the company, including JP Morgan and the Jane Street Group, both of which have purchased ZYNE stock in the past 6 months. These are small positions however so I wouldn't get too excited off the back of this fact. Institutions now own just over 20% of ZYNE's shares.

As such, ZYNE is probably the most high risk stock out of the ones discussed in this section. That means it's fairly valued, but there is a built-in risk profile that cannot be ignored. At this point, it's really a race against time to get approval for either ZYN001 and/or ZYN002. GWPH already have first mover advantage for CBD drugs, so ZYNE has a lot of catching up to do. However, the rewards for this one will be great, if approval occurs. To reiterate again, you must be able to tolerate risk if you decide to invest in ZYNE, if you can't allow that much potential downside in your portfolio, then stay on the sidelines for this one.

Canopy Growth Corporation ($CGC)

Stephen Satoshi

Price at time of writing: $40.08

The second Canadian marijuana company to be listed on the New York Stock Exchange, Canopy's May listing is just another sign the world's largest marijuana company goes from strength to strength. Initially listed with a market cap of $5.7 billion, that number is now around the $8 billion range.

Reaching an all time high of over $40/share, the move came after an announcement by Constellation Brands that it had increased its stake in the company by over $4 billion. This makes Constellation the single biggest shareholder.

They boast some of the largest production facilities in the world, with over 6 million square feet of growing space. With retail operations in Canada (but not the US due to their NYSE listing) and across the globe, this is a truly international company, with German revenue accounting for around 10% of their bottom line. There are also plans to target market in Colombia, Chile, Brazil and Australia in the coming years. Perhaps interestingly enough, the US retail market is fairly low on their priority levels due to the company's relatively negative outlook on US federal legalization.

So the biggest question with Canopy is as follows - if it's already the biggest company in the market, how big can it get? Personally, I'm extremely bullish on the company, their CEO Bruce Linton is a visionary in this area, who sees the company as more than just a strict marijuana company. If Canopy can further disrupt the pharmaceutical and alcohol industries, then the sky really is the limit. Then you have the possibility of a full blown takeover by Constellation or another Big Alcohol company, although I personally think the possibility of this is somewhat overstated.

Another reason I like Linton's outlook is that he is not focused on the tobacco market as competition, in his own words *"We're not really a substitute for nicotine. If you're hooked on nicotine, you're hooked on nicotine."* Many other analysts look at this competition as too literal, namely, they are both things you can smoke, ergo they must be in direct competition with one another. However, consumer behavior indicates that this is not the case. Therefore the alcohol comparison makes a lot more sense in my view.

As previously discussed, Canopy is leading the charge for international expansion. In the past 5 years alone, we have seen the number of countries discussing marijuana legalization on a federal level increase from 4 to 29, and Canopy sees this as one of its biggest opportunities going forward. The downside to this is that for a lot of these countries, the demand levels for medical and recreational cannabis have not been truly assessed and are just predictions at this stage.

Note: The listed for Canopy Growth on the Toronto Stock Exchange use the $WEED ticker

CannTrust Holdings ($CNTTF)

Price at time of writing: $6.39

CannTrust holding is in a unique position in that it is one of the view marijuana companies which is profitable right here and now. What is also unique is that it's one of the few marijuana stocks to experience a drop in share price this year, so what's going on at the Canadian marijuana grower?

The company's main assets are two production facilities which have 500,000 square feet of combined growing space. A construction of a third growing facility will see them able to reach their end goal of a yield topping 100,000KG a year. A diverse business model sees CannTrust producing dry flowers, pre-rolled joints, oils and extracts.

The firm has produced 3 profitable quarters in a row, mainly fueled by solid sales numbers in its extracts and oils business. Year to date growth is up over 100% and the grower also boasts a forward price to earnings (a better indicator in a high growth market than regular P/E) ratio of 24, which in layman's terms indicates that the stock is fairly valued when you factor in future profitability. It's also one of the few marijuana companies with more cash in hand than long term debts ($11.7m vs. $9.5m)

Yet despite all this, share prices are down due to increased competition in the space and increased pressure on smaller growers like CannTrust. It's really a case of, can a small company with low operating costs and a business model focused on incremental growth, really compete with some of the giants in the industry like Canopy? On the domestic side of things, supply will eventually catch up to demand in the next 3 years, and thus there simply won't be enough room for all these Canadian growers.

Does that mean you should count CannTrust out of the marijuana race? Not necessarily.

The company is not just focused on the domestic front and has already agreed deals with Australian and Denmark authorities to ship medical marijuana to those countries. Further agreements with Brazil, Mexico and Germany are planned in the near term future. This represents somewhat of a hedge against a potentially dwindling domestic market, but not too much of an overshoot that is could adversely affect prices if demand in Europe doesn't meet projections. In short, it's a good middle ground for the company to have.

Other future plans include looking at the potential in the medical marjuana for pets. The company recently announced a partnership with Grey Wolf Animal Health. While this market is projected to be small initially, it will represent an additional revenue stream for the Canadian firm.

Overall, based on its current price in relation to overall profitability levels, CannTrust seems to be one of few marijuana companies which could be considered undervalued at the time of the writing. There are certain drawbacks that these smaller marijuana growers have, but in the short to medium term, this one appears to be an attractive investment.

ETFMJ Alternative Harvest ETF ($MJ)

Price at time of writing: $32.54

One of the more stranger financial tales told in this marijuana stock boom, the ETFMG Alternative Harvest ETF was one that quickly took shape after it became apparent that marijuana stocks weren't just a short term play.

Previously a middling ETF focusing on Latin American real estate, within 3 months it had completely shifted its focus onto the weed market. At one point in January, the ETF had a higher trading volume than the iShares S&P 500 ETF, which just goes to show how big the marijuana market has become in such a short space of time.

It should be noted that the fund is made up of stocks which are not considered strict marijuana ones like Scotts Miracle Gro (some marijuana based revenue from subsidiaries) and Philip Morris International (no marijuana revenue as yet, but may expand into the market in the future).

Currently, its two biggest holding are Canopy Growth, Cronos Group and Aurora Cannabis, which is what you would expect from the premiere marijuana ETF.

So is this ETF right for you if you don't want to invest in individual companies? Well, the answer lies in your risk profile. While this is arguably the least volatile way to gain exposure to the marijuana market, there are still some potential drawbacks. For example, many of the fund's holdings are still in unprofitable companies, which is something you will have to monitor in the next 6-12 months. The fund is rebalanced quarterly, but that still leaves you exposed to short term price movements.

The fund does have a fee of 0.75%, which is quite high for an ETF. Most sector tracking ETFs have fees around 0.25%. However as this is still a somewhat volatile industry, with a number of stocks trading on different exchanges, I feel the fee is justified.

I should also note that any stock performance before December 26th 2017 can be ignored as this was when the fund traded Latin American real estate and therefore this part of its portfolio is no longer valid.

Cronos Group ($CRON)

Price at time of writing: $7.96

To cap off a phenomenal year, in February, Cronos became the first Canadian marijuana grower to be listed on the NASDAQ. This will shortly be followed by the official opening of the nationwide legal marijuana market in Canada this coming October. However, for Cronos, as well as other stocks mentioned in this book, it's not just Canada which is poised to fuel growth going forward.

The group's core business as of right now comes from the sale of medical marijuana to licensed distributors around Canada. It continues to bring on new patients at a rapid rate, which has pushed the stock's price higher and higher in the past 12 months. How high you ask? How does 250% growth sound to you? But if you think the best days are behind you, or that it's too late to get a piece of Cronos going forward, I respectfully disagree, because this stock has a long way to go.

An often overlooked point among analysts, and one thing to note about a stock like Cronos, is that as of June 2018, Canadian banks can now lend money to marijuana companies without consequence. This is a huge victory for how companies like Cronos go about their day to day business. If you've read my first book on this subject, you'll remember I noted that one of the main challenges facing marijuana companies is the lack of banking structure that was available to them. Now, this has changed, it leaves a clear path for these companies to further grow as we move forward.

The company posted stunning year on year growth of 234% during its Q2 earnings call. Perhaps even more impressive, gross profit rose by 466% in this same time period. This is largely due to the domestic (Canadian in the case of Cronos) marijuana market. With new federal level legalization North of the border projected to bring in more than $5 billion CAD in extra revenue, Cronos is poised for a strong near future.

The company is ramping up its production capacity and plans to go from 6,600KG a year at present to more than 40,000KG a year within 12 months. Much of this expansion is down to joint ventures with other growers.

The group's US prospects are also looking good as the company recently partnered with US firm MedMen in an agreement which will see additional retail marijuana stores launched throughout Canada.

In terms of a global presence, Cronos has operations in Germany, Australia and also in Poland. A big factor in future success will be how much penetration they can get into the European market. This is a crowded space and one where first mover advantage will be more apparent than ever. Rival firm Tilray currently has agreements in place to distribute marijuana in Portugal, which is a much faster growing market than that of Germany and Poland. This battle for European dominance is one area to watch when deciding between marijuana stocks.

The stock may also emerge as a takeover target for a big alcohol company (more on this later in the book). This kind of institutional level investment signals big price movements in favor of those already holding it. Cronos isn't alone in being a takeover target, but it is one of the firms with enough of a foundation in place where it appeals to investment from outside the marijuana industry.

10 Exciting Marijuana Penny Stocks Currently Trading Under $1

Before we begin, I should make a general disclaimer about penny stocks.

If you have not invested in them before, penny stocks are a high risk proposition. The vast majority of penny stocks are in a position where the company is losing money in its present day state.

For many of these companies, it is a case of finding their big break (whether that is a takeover, a partnership or a breakthrough) before they run of a cash and have to go under.

As such, do not invest more than a small portion of your portfolio into these penny stocks.

For further clarification, I have listed their US ticker codes next to the stocks in question, plus double check that these are the same if you are outside the United States.

Sunset Island Group Inc. ($SIGO)

Price at time of writing: $0.44

A stock that's currently trading 60% down from its all time high might not seem like a likely candidate for this book, but there are certain things about Sunset Island Group which mean you can't count out the company yet.

It received its growing and cultivation license in January and its location in California makes it primed to capitalize on the growing recreational marijuana market in the Golden State.

The company plans to expand to over 750,000 square feet of growing space. Much of this expansion will be funded by equity agreements rather than the toxic debt which so many other penny stocks rely on to get to their one big breakthrough. They have also promised no share dilution either.

SIGO also has a diversified product line including pre-rolled marijuana cigarettes in addition to the dry flowers it grows and them sells to dispensaries.

Overall it's worth taking a look into this California grower, purely because of their ambitious management team and aggressive expansion plans.

Easton Pharmaceuticals Inc. ($EAPH)

Price at time of writing: $0.02

A pharmaceutical company with a difference in that its products are more focused on the general consumer market than any specific disease prevention or cure. Easton has already developed a Cannabis based motion sickness get known as Nauseogel and also has an anti-aging skincare cream called Skin Renou HA.

Easton also has plans to invest in a large casino and hotel resort in Europe. Gaming is a growth industry and the move could well pay off. However, it remains to be seen what kind of financial obligation this leaves Easton in the short term and if that obligation will prevent growth from its core cannabis business. Some investors have speculated that this a pre-emptive move to be able to sell marijuana directly to casino go-ers. That seems like a stretch right now seeing as the country the casino will be built in is yet to be confirmed. If indeed that is the case though, this is an intriguing angle to take on a fast growing market like the legal marijuana one. This stock is worth monitoring for sure.

Medical Marijuana Inc. ($MJNA)

Price at time of writing: $0.10

One of the more well known small cap companies in this book. MJNA was the first publicly traded marijuana stock and producers a variety of a CBD based products. It also owns a number of subsidiary companies including branches of its HempMeds brand in Mexico and Brazil.

I've previously discussed how CBD products have higher profit margins than dried marijuana flowers, so MJNA has that going for it. Plus the foot holding in Brazil and Mexico make for good international expansion potential in the future.

I should also note that MJNA owns roughly 40% of AXIM, another smallcap marijuana company. AXIM is a pharmaceutical firm who are currently going through some rough patches with clinical trials for CBD based drugs. A potential red flag here is that MJNA is profitable while AXIM is not. Therefore a lot of MJNA's short term growth may lay in just how profitable (or not) AXIM can be.

mCig Inc. ($MCIG)

Price at time of writing: $0.34

A small cannabis grower and greenhouse construction company, but one you shouldn't count out.

One thing I particularly like about mCig is their aims to diversify as part of a medium term risk mitigation strategy. Not just relying on increasing square footage to drive growth, the company is also expanding into areas like CBD production, cannabis technology and medicinal development. This leaves it less exposed to risks such as oversupply or getting priced out of the market by the larger producers.

One other interesting area of potential growth is in its eHESIVE advertising network. This is a platform which will allow advertisers on the internet to target cannabis users. This is a great short term play because larger advertising platforms like Facebook and Google AdWords do not allow any kind of marijuana relating advertisements at the time of writing. So eHESIVE allows marijuana companies to get additional market penetration and thus have additional traffic driven to their respective websites.

Cannex Capital Holdings Inc ($CNXXF)

Price at time of writing: $0.87

Already the owner of largest marijuana producer in Washington state, this small cap holding company has far bigger ambitions.

The company is expanding into other states on the West Coast. An expansion into California is one that will continue to grow the company beyond its current state.

An acquisition of Jetty Extracts gives Cannex extra exposure to the growing vaporizer market as well. This particular play is one I like a lot and should be looked at a massive positive for Cannex going forward. 50% of new marijuana customers are vaporizer users as opposed to ones who smoke dry flowers. Therefore in a growing market, which will see lots more first time users, Cannex will likely benefit from this additional customer base.

More acquisitions are needed if Cannex is to keep up with some of the larger companies In the space, but CEO Anthony Dutton has a solid vision for short to medium term growth, which is why I like this particular small cap so much.

It should be noted that Cannex is a pure holding company, so it does provide funding to the companies it owns and does it get involved in the day to day running of said companies.

CROP Infrastructure Corp ($CRXPF)

Price at time of writing: $0.16

Crop Corp is another multi-faceted marijuana company. The Canadian firm owns marijuana based properties, has a construction arm which builds large indoor growing operations and also provides agricultural equipment to new marijuana companies.

This turnkey approach allows them to partner with new growers who have just had their license approved. Which in turn allows the growers to get a running start without having to invest large amounts of initial capital.

One potential growth area is in the expanding European market. The company just partnered with Italian firm XHemplar on what can only be considered a mega plantation.

The 522,000 square foot facility will be 30% owned by Crop and will be the largest in Italy. The facility is expected to yield around 44,000 pounds of low THC, high CBD cannabis in the first year of operations. If you aren't too familiar with the industry, that's a huge amount.

Italy has been somewhat of a trailblazer when it comes to marijuana in the European market. It has been legal for medical use since 2006 and demand was actually outstripping supply until recently. As such, much of the country's medical marijuana had to be imported from the Netherlands and oddly enough, Canada. Overall consumptions levels have increased nearly tenfold in the past 4 years, and the European nation shows no signs of slowing down any time soon.

As Europe continues to recognize the medicinal benefits of marijuana, partnerships like this for US and Canadian companies will be invaluable in fueling expansion outside of the crowded domestic market. At its current price CROP looks like a decent play based off this Italian deal alone, and further domestic progress could see this penny stock move into the big leagues sooner rather than later.

Mountain High Acquisitions Corp. ($MYHI)

Price at time of writing: $0.07

Another holding company, and one which helps provide cannabis providers with the necessary funding to grow their business.

One of their projects, a pilot initiative alongside D9 Manufacturing, aims to help cannabis producers increase their yield per square footage. In other words, they will decrease the number of bad crops per year. This is a unique strategy in a sector where a lot of companies are focused purely on having the largest square footage growth sites. One of efficiency rather than brute force and something that could be extremely beneficial as this microcap looks to grow in the next 18-24 months.

One thing to note is that this a particularly low volume stock, and as such, is susceptible to manipulation from larger traders. This shouldn't be a concern as the stock grows but is something you should keep tabs on for a few days before deciding to pull the trigger.

Newgen Concepts Inc. ($VPOR)

Price at time of writing: $0.0006

An intriguing stock, and the lowest priced one in this entire book.

Perhaps most well known for their Easy Grinder line of herbal grinders. This dual automatic and manual grinder is a favorite among users who prefer dry marijuana flowers. For those unaware, it is necessary to use a grinder to make the dry marijuana flowers the right size to wrap in paper or pack into a pipe. It also has uses in cannabis baking. Last year the group signed their first overseas distribution deal with Dutch firm Simply Green.

Their newly formed subsidiary, Royal CBD will help them penetrate further into the CBD market, which is one that has shown tremendous potential in the past few months. CBD is an easier sell than regular marijuana as it does not have any psychoactive effects like THC based products. As such, it is popular with first time cannabis users and demographics which don't usually gravitate towards the marijuana market.

One of the struggles they face in the short term is a classic penny stock case of if they can become profitable or not. They previously sold one of their other subsidiaries Simple Cork Inc. to the Rich Cigars Inc. Then used the proceeds of this sale to pay off $2 million outstanding debt. Obviously, this isn't a pattern which can be continuously replicated and as such, profitably will need to come from other areas of the company.

Note: Newgen was previously known as VaporGroup Inc.

Player's Network ($PNTV)

Price at time of writing: $0.058

Now licensed in 2 separate states, Player's Network is potential marijuana pure play in the next 12 months. By pure play I mean the firm primarily focuses on the growing and selling of marijuana rather than any logistics type business.

They also own WeedTV which is an online social network and lifestyle channel designed for marijuana enthusiasts. This is a useful asset to have because it provides traffic to PNTV's holdings as well as benefitting from ad revenue from other companies looking to get more exposure for their brand.

The firm recently announced their best ever month in terms of sales as well, which is a solid sign that they are trending in the right direction.

The company also recently acquired Green Leaf Farms Salinas Valley, which gives them more total square footage in their operations. In an online webinar, the firm continued to reiterate its growth by acquisition strategy, which while aggressive, is somewhat necessary for a competitive landscape like this one. Green Lead manufactures both dry flowers as well as other cannabis products like oils and extracts.

Golden Leaf Holdings Ltd. ($GLDFF)

Price at time of writing: $0.20

It's not very often that a company aims to be the McDonald's of it industry, but that's exactly what Golden Leaf Holdings is trying to do.

The company's ultimate goal is a set of brand name franchises across the US, Canada and beyond. Management believes that by having a trusted name, customers can rely on a consistent flower and product quality across the entire world. This makes sense in a market where small producers often struggle to guarantee quality time and time again. It's an audacious plan, but one I like. This could be especially beneficial in expanding markets where a solid brand name has more chance of winning over the local customers than a company which no one has ever heard of.

Golden Leaf announced a takeover of Nevada based Tahoe Hydroponics in August 2018, a power move which shows their determination to scale quickly in the next 18-24 months. Tahoe has brand name recognition in the industry and this takeover was somewhat of a surprise, considering that they were rumours swirling of one of the larger companies in the industry looking to buy them out. Quite the coup for GLDFF. Tahoe gives GLDFF exposure to markets in both Nevada and California and gives the Canadian firm a strong entry into the US market. One thing I like about the deal is that the two top Tahoe executives will stay on for 18 months to oversee the transition. A big problem with firms going into international markets is lack of local expertise and Tahoe's guys will provide this in the short term.

Plus one marijuana penny stock to avoid…

Cannabis Science Inc. ($CBIS)

Price at time of writing: $0.055

A small biotech company based out of California, Cannabis Science Inc. Should be avoided, but not for any marijuana related reasons. The CEO Raymond C. Dabney is named in a lawsuit filed by the SEC, which accused him of manipulating stock prices. He has also been barred from serving as an officer or director of a company in Canada.

Either way, stay well away from this one.

Non-Marijuana Companies who could profit from the coming boom

While there are many companies who could benefit from an increased marijuana market, there are 3 in particular which I wanted to spotlight here.

These are 4 companies which you would not expect to be affected by marijuana, and you might have no idea that they were even involved in the marijuana industry.

Constellation Brands ($STZ)

Price at time of writing: $211.22

The well known brewer, who owns such beer brands as Corona and Modelo, is making its move into the marijuana market.

It's a pretty simple equation, the US beer market is steadily declining, and the Canadian market is plummeting at an even faster rate. Cannabis is the next big thing and thus the marriage was an obvious one.

The company added $3.8 billion worth of Canopy Growth shares in August, taking their total ownership to 38%. This could rise to above 50% if STZ exercises all of its warrants as part of the terms of the deal. This move is expected to result in Constellation and Canopy producing a line of cannabis infused beverages. I should note that it is unlikely these will be alcoholic. It's also likely that these beverages will be sold overseas as well, although the US and Canada will obviously be the focus in the early stages of this joint venture.

Constellation is one of the few beverage companies which isn't experiencing stagnated growth, so there are unlikely to be any setbacks with the partnership. Both the Corona and Modelo brands are gaining market share and are making in-roads against the traditional favorites like

Budweiser and Coors. STZ also has a great track record of capital investment, and their latest move looks like it is going to continue this.

Canada's Molson Coors is also entering the space, and others are expected to join, so it is definitely a race to see who can corner the cannabis beverage market first. Heineken have already developed a cannabis infused sparkling water drink with California's Lagunitas brewery.

This is one stock I'd be very confident holding in the long term. You won't get the kind of massive growth that is possible with some of the marijuana pure plays, but it does offer a solid entry point into the industry without the volatility of some of the other stocks discussed in this book.

Scott's Miracle-Gro ($SMG)

Price at time of writing: $74.69

One of the best stories to come out of 2017 was when the mainstream financial media starting picking up on Scott's Miracle Gro owning a marijuana based subsidiary. This was one of those lightbulb moments which put "pot stocks" firmly in the eyes of regular investors. While the marijuana subsidiary Hawthorne Gardening is not a huge part of SMG's bottom line, it is still something we should look at.

There are a number of hurdles to overcome with regards to Hawthorne's products and their legality in the US. However, it does represent a nice bit of diversification for the company. Gardening has long been a seasonal industry with an ageing customer base. Opening up to marijuana, which is both non-seasonal and attracts a younger demographic, is a great hedge for SMG.

This is a stock I'm slightly less bullish on than in my first book on the subject. This is mainly due to a recent call with CEO Jim Hagedorn. Hagedorn discussed that Hawthorne Gardening wasn't meeting internal targets, and is unlikely to for the forseeable future. Hawthrone is also in the process of acquiring Sunlight Supply, and projections will likely be revised after that acquisition is complete. Either way, it's a rocky start for Scott's marijuana arm.

Scott's is down 28% on the year, mainly due to investors being too confident in the January marijuana boom. Some analysts are now very bearish on the stock as a result, Zacks.com even went as far as to call it their Bear of The Day in late August. However, I feel the current price represents a good entry level for investors who are in this for the long haul. Let me be clear about SMG, this is a mature company, and one which isn't going to provide an overnight 2 or 3X. But it is a solid hold for those looking at building a futureproof portfolio. Overall, despite the challenge for SMG going forward, I still like the company, and its core business is strong enough to offset any marijuana based headaches in the short term at least.

Cree Inc. ($CREE)

Price at time of writing: $47.55

Now I know what you're thinking, what does an LED lighting company have to do with the cannabis industry?

Well, the answer is simple, LED bulbs are a vital component of the indoor marijuana growing process. Roughly 1/3 of all US marijuana is grown indoors. Right now, many small growers currently favor HPS bulbs because of their lower upfront costs. However, HPS bulbs, while powerful, burn out quickly and eat up a lot of electricity. A full scale industry switch to LED would mean big things for companies like CREE.

What is interesting though is that while CREE admits that part of its business is derived from the marijuana industry, just what percentage of its bottom line this represents remains somewhat of a mystery. However, if the previous paragraph does indeed come true, CREE is one of the companies set to profit most from the move.

22nd Century Group ($XXII)

Price at time of writing: $2.39

It might be surprising to see a stock mentioned that's up nearly 150% this year alone, but this is one particular company which has potential to rise far, far above its current position.

22ⁿᵈ Century Group's future potential depends largely on the Food and Drug Administration (FDA). The FDA wants to lower the nicotine content in cigarettes, in order to make them less addictive to the masses. 22ⁿᵈ Century happens to be the leading manufacturer of low nicotine cigarettes in the country.

I should note at the outset of this analysis, that this is not a marijuana company, and these are not marijuana cigarettes, this is a strict tobacco product. The company *is* involved in the development of cannabis plants with zero THC levels, but that is not where their short term future relies on right now.

The company owns a patent (well, 4 actually) with 20 year exclusivity for what is known as Modified Risk Tobacco Products (RFTPs), this particular tobacco crop could replace regular cigarettes. This patent gives them, what is essentially a monopoly on this entire space. Before you dump your retirement fund into this particular stock though, there are a couple of hurdles still to overcome.

The future success of the company is largely dependent on whether 22ⁿᵈ Century is allowed to market this kind of cigarette as being "less harmful" than the regular variety. Previous attempts by tobacco companies to do this have been nixed by the FDA. This includes both cigarettes and in the marketing of electronic cigarettes or vape pens.

In terms of competition, you'd have to look to Big Tobacco for that, by 22ⁿᵈ Century has first mover advantage in this respect. British American Tobacco ($BAT) has previously stated that it would take them over 20 years to mass produce the amounts of low nicotine tobacco needed to meet potential demand. Philip Morris ($PM), another tobacco giant has similar sentiments regarding its own production of low nicotine tobacco. However, in the short term, 22nd Century could profit by licensing out seeds to these and other Big Tobacco firms.

It's not just the US that matters in this overall equation though, the Chinese cigarette market is roughly 30% of the entire population. That's over 500 million people, more than 100 million more people than the entire population of the United States.

The big question is whether 22nd Century can find a way around the FDA's stubborn stance on labelling. As far as the FDA is concerned in its current position, cigarettes are dangerous and cancer causing, and simply lowering their nicotine content does nothing to correct this in the short term. However, if the FDA forces the tobacco industry to adopt this low nicotine tobacco going forward, then 22nd Century has huge advantages in this respect. If you're willing to accept that the company may peeter out into nothing, then this is worth a speculative play based on a huge reward if it does pay off.

When looking at financials, the company posted a $19 million loss in the past 12 months, not uncommon for a smaller company in this space. To reiterate though, you are not buying this stock based on current performance, this is purely based on a bright future.

In terms of portfolio diversification, you should look at 22nd Century Group as a biotech stock rather than a tobacco or consumable company, as their short term strengths lie largely in their patents rather than any hard assets.

Can non-Canadian residents buy Canadian stocks?

As you may have seen, a large number of these stocks are listed on the Toronto Stock Exchange, Canada's largest stock exchange. Some are also listed on US regulated exchanges, which means you can buy them using a local broker, or broker who supports US stocks if you are based outside of the US.

You can also buy certain Canadian stocks from many online brokerage houses including TD Ameritrade, Schwab and E-Trade. I should note though, these stocks may have higher commissions than US stocks when using these sites. Some of the commissions can be as high as $19 per trade. I advise you to check your broker's rates for Canadian stocks. This task would be made easier by calling them on the phone rather than trying to dig through their respective website looking for rates. At the time of writing, only Schwab uses the same rates for both US and Canadian stocks.

It should be noted that some online brokers do not directly buy Canadian stocks, they instead purchase pink sheets as a proxy for the stock. These pink sheets will have a 1:1 value, but trading volume will be lower than the volume on Canadian exchanges. So this is something to look out for if you are planning on buying or selling large amounts, and I would always recommend double checking with your broker before executing any trades.

The other thing to note is if you are using a US broker, you may be looking for a different stock symbol than the ones listed in this book. These symbols will usually be 5 letters long, so make sure to check your particular stock's corresponding US symbol before you accidentally buy shares of the wrong company.

Conclusion

Well, there we have it, an overview of the exciting marijuana stocks sector, and the potential benefits of investing in it. Like I said before, projections have been revised and this market is now projected to increase fivefold in the next decade. Meaning there is enormous opportunity across many different areas of the industry. From growing to manufacturing and distribution and real estate, marijuana is going to make a lot of people rich in the next few years. The question is, will you be one of them?

Like any high growth industry, there is an amount of risk involved when investing. Therefore I urge you to do additional research on top of what you've read in this book. There are also a number of external factors to consider, many of these are out of the control of the companies they will affect so it would be wise to monitor any legalization news closely. Both at a state level and at a federal one.

Marijuana is still in the early stages as an asset class, so as such many of these companies should be looked at as more speculative plays, similar to cryptocurrency in this respect (albeit with far less volatility). This also means they should not make up a significant portion of your portfolio.

I hope you've enjoyed what you have read in this book, and if you do decide to invest in marijuana stocks, I hope you make a lot of money.

Thanks,

Stephen Satoshi

Marijuana Stocks

Beginners Guide To The Only Industry Producing Financial

Returns as Fast as Cryptocurrency

By

Stephen Satoshi

Introduction

Outside of cryptocurrency, the marijuana industry in the fastest growing asset class on Earth. In 2017 alone it grew by more than 30%.

That growth is showing no signs of slowing down and legal marijuana is projected to be a near $25 billion industry in the US alone by 2020. Between the US and Canadian stock exchanges, there are now over 220 securities which can broadly be described as "marijuana stocks".

And that's even with the US federal government listing Marijuana as a schedule 1 drug. That's in the same category as cocaine and methamphetamine. It may also surprise you to discover that despite this rapid boom, there is still only 1 single federally approved growing facility in the entire United States.

However, a number of factors in the coming year indicate that this is all about to change.

You see, 29 states now allow legal use of marijuana for recreational purposes, medical purposes, or both.

And the ball is already rolling for further state by state legalization.

64% of US citizens now support legalizing the drug nationwide, that's compared to just 25% when the same question was asked in 1995. 70% of citizens are opposed to a federal marijuana crackdown, according to a poll conducted by Vice. Among younger people, that number is now at a staggeringly high 94%. It goes without saying that the average American's view of marijuana has drastically changed in the past 20 years.

Nationwide legalization of medical marijuana in the USA is now a matter of *when* not if.

And that's not even considering Canada's move to legalize recreational marijuana. The country has already legalized medical marijuana nationwide, and this next move could have an even bigger effect on the market as a whole once the bill passes, which is currently projected to be in the summer of 2018. Canada has its own list of marijuana stocks which offer a tremendous money making opportunity.

No wonder it's been dubbed "the green rush".

Marijuana doesn't just have great investment potential, there are a huge number of economic and social benefits as well. The positive effects are already being seen in early adopter states like Colorado. The first state to approve recreational marijuana use, saw a 30% year-on-year rise in legal sales since 2012. This resulted in $200 million extra dollars in the state's bottom line from tax revenue. Colorado is using this money for good, as much of the money is being reinvested into educational programs and drug-abuse initiatives.

These are exciting times ahead for marijuana both on a medical and recreational level. And there are so many different ways to profit from this. These aren't just limited to the growers and distributors of the plant. Everything from real estate to biotech to a company that manufacturers tiny plastic tubes will be covered in this book. We'll also be doing an analysis of 12 different highlighted marijuana stocks and their different business models.

I hope you enjoy this book and that the information inside proves valuable to you.

Thanks,

Stephen

So just *how* legal is marijuana these days?

One of the more confusing elements of the booming marijuana industry is the legality of it all. In the USA, while marijuana is still illegal at a federal level, different types of marijuana availability is decided on a state by state basis.

As previously noted, recreational marijuana, available to anyone over the age of 21 in the same vein as alcohol is currently legal in 8 states. Medical marijuana, available to anyone over the age of 21 with a doctor's prescription, is legal in 29 states. Now here's where it gets confusing with medical marijuana is being illegal at a federal level. So technically, possessing marijuana is still a federal crime in these states, even if you have a medical marijuana card. This leads to some confusing legislature such as jobs being able to fire employees for off-the-clock marijuana use. Landlords can also evict tenants for marijuana use, even if their state allows it. What we should be concerned with most as an investor is the main law that affects medical marijuana companies. This is the law that means many of these companies cannot get access to full banking and credit due to the federally illegal nature of their business, the law was put into place to prevent drug dealers from laundering money through banks. We'll be going on to discuss how this affects marijuana businesses later on in this book.

Below is a full breakdown of the exact legality of marijuana and cannabinoids on a state-by-state basis.

States That Have Legalized Industrial Hemp Production

- Alabama, Arkansas, California, Colorado, Florida, Georgia, Hawaii, Illinois, Indiana, Kentucky, Maine, Michigan, Minnesota, Mississippi, Montana, Nebraska, Nevada, New Hampshire, North Carolina, North Dakota, Oregon, Pennsylvania, Rhode Island, South Carolina, Tennessee, Utah, Vermont, Virginia, Washington and Wyoming.

States That Have Legalized Hemp Oil/CBD Hemp Oil

- Legal in all fifty states, though CBD Hemp oil is still illegal in Idaho, Indiana, Kansas, Nebraska, South Dakota and West Virginia.

States That Have Legalized Medicinal Marijuana

- Alaska, Arizona, Arkansas, California, Colorado, Connecticut, Delaware, Florida, Hawaii, Illinois, Maine, Maryland, Massachusetts, Michigan, Minnesota, Montana, Nevada, New Hampshire, New Jersey, New Mexico, New York, North Dakota, Ohio, Oregon, Pennsylvania, Rhode Island, Vermont, Washington, Washington DC and West Virginia.

States That Have Legalized Recreational Use of Marijuana

- Alaska, California, Colorado, Maine, Massachusetts, Nevada, Oregon and Washington.

It is also predicted that a further 5 states: Vermont, New Jersey, Michigan, Oklahoma and Utah - will each legalize adult recreational marijuana by the end of 2018.

Supply and Demand

One obvious, yet often overlooked factor in the marijuana market is the supply and demand of the plant. This has historically been difficult to quantify due to the previous illegality of the drug, and thus a lack of consistent evidence. Many investors naturally assume that legalization across more and more states will lead to increased demand, which is true.

However, something that is also true is that supply is actually outstripping demand. For example, in California, locally grown supplies are up threefold from 2006 to a staggering 13.5 million pounds a year. In the past 2 years, the wholesale price of marijuana has plunged from around $2,100 per pound to $1,600 per pound. This is not only due to increased competition as more and more growers enter the market every year. There is also the technological advancement in growing techniques, which is further lowering wholesale prices. Great for the consumer, but obviously not so great for the growing companies. Until federal nationwide legalization, it is also difficult for these growers to be able to sell their excess harvest to other states due to the different laws in place. Therefore there is no option to take advantage of geographical arbitrage by growing in states with lower land prices, then selling in states with wealthier consumers.

The interesting caveat to this is that the current fear North of the border in Canada, is that supply will not be able to meet demand is nationwide legalization does occur in the summer of 2018 as is expected. Current estimates don't favor producers, and many believe that it will be at least 2 years before they are able to consistently meet the demand for marijuana across the country. Other estimates are less optimistic and have this figure at nearer 4 years before demand can be met. Marijuana producers are scrambling to agree on a deal on a state-by-state basis and we are also seeing companies work together in order to try and streamline their processes so they can meet demand.

Marijuana Real Estate

It's not just growers and sellers that are profiting from this "green rush", the real estate market is being turned on its head. As more than 20 states have legalized medical marijuana, as a result, an under reported yet significant part boom is the form of real estate. This being the land that marijuana growers, factories and stores utilize. Even celebrities are getting involved, including former Heavyweight Champion boxer Mike Tyson has just purchased a 40-acre ranch in a remote California which will be dedicated to growing operations, as well as a luxury marijuana resort for cannabis enthusiasts. Tyson plans to use the ranch to provide jobs for military veterans in the local community.

You see, Cannabis sales are higher per square foot than department stores by 5 to 1. Drug stores by 1.5 to 1, and narrowly beating out Whole Foods. In fact, Marijuana sales per square foot are closer to that of Costco than any other entity. This combined with the numerous red tape and bureaucracy that marijuana businesses face has led to a significant premium in the average price of real estate for a marijuana business versus a conventional business.

For example, in Denver, the marijuana industry pays on average a 50% premium for warehouse buildings. Sometimes this premium can as much as 2 or even 3 times higher than non-marijuana businesses! Colorado is one of the big winners when it comes to the marijuana real estate boom, and over one third of new industrial tenants are now marijuana businesses.

The biggest opportunities to be had is in states that newly legalize medical and recreational marijuana use. For example, states like Michigan and New Jersey both of whom are on the brink of legalization. However, bills can stall, as we have seen in states like Maine. So, therefore, there is a significant element of risk in trying to "jump the gun" and get a head start on the marijuana real estate boom. There is also the issue of zoning laws and the areas that these businesses are allowed to operate in.

One interesting potential development is how federal legalization would impact real estate with regards to interstate transportation. Right now, all legal marijuana sold within that state must be grown in the same state in avoid to not violate federal drug trafficking laws. However, a nationwide legalization would result in this not applying, and thus companies could take advantage of parts of the country with lower land prices. The biggest losers in this scenario would be East Coast producers who traditionally have the highest land prices of all the legal marijuana states.

This isn't the first time real estate has made its mark in an unfamiliar industry. Let's take a look at McDonald's for instance. Not only is McDonald's and its' Golden Arches one of America's most iconic companies, it's also one of the best performing stocks of the last 30 years. Outperforming IBM and Coca-Cola over the same time period. Many investors shun McDonald's for its low-cost, low-brow business model of offering cheap food to the masses. However, what people really overlook is the *business* of McDonald's.

You see, in investment terms, McDonald's is really a real estate company. A large chunk of their annual profits comes from buying land cheaply, then leasing it at higher prices to its franchisees. One of the simplest business models imaginable, but one that has continued to produce profits, hand over foot, for the past 50 years. Founder Ray Kroc was even quoted as saying "We are in the real estate business, not the hamburger business."

And now, the marijuana industry is undergoing a similar phenomenon. Marijuana businesses are prevented from receiving bank loan or mortgages under federal law. Therefore, nearly all marijuana businesses are forced to rent their buildings at a premium. So it is the landlords who are making a killing off of this.

We've even seen support from institutional investors, in January, a little known ETF, the ETFMG Alternative Harvest ETF moved its focus from Latin American real estate to the thriving marijuana industry. The fund made some big plays, including acquiring over 300,000 shares of Turning Point Brands.

Although it should be noted that the majority of Alternative Harvest holdings are in the growing and distribution sector, that doesn't mean more of a real estate based portfolio can't be counted out in the future. After all, their initial focus was on the Latin American real estate market, so the fund managers have previous expertise in that sector.

It's large swings in focus like what we have seen from Alternative Harvest that indicate that the market is undergoing something of a boom. We may well see further emphasis on this sector as we move forward into 2018 and beyond. Needless to say, there is a certain hysteria around marijuana real estate right now, and many investors are clamoring to get their piece of the pie.

Big Tobacco vs. Cannabis Industry

Big Tobacco is one of the main detractors from the medical marijuana industry. This is the same set of companies that vehemently denied for years that tobacco was dangerous to one's health. It was only the result of a multi-state lawsuit that got them to do so. Funnily enough, there were reports of the tobacco industry gearing up for legalized marijuana as far back as the 1970s. There is even a handwritten memo from the President of Philip Morris Tobacco George Weissman stating "While I am opposed to its use, I recognize that it may be legalized in the near future...Thus, with these great auspices, we should be in a position to examine: 1. A potential competition, 2. A possible product, 3. At this time, cooperate with the government." Philip Morris also formally requested marijuana samples from the Department of Justice so they could carry out their own testing.

The more intriguing part of this memo is the section saying "We are in the business of relaxing people who are tense and providing a pick up for people who are bored or depressed. The human needs that our product fills will not go away. **Thus, the only real threat to our business is that society will find other means of satisfying these needs.**" The last sentence is where the cannabis industry comes into play. Will tobacco companies actively try to put a stop to increasing legalization, rather than trying to enter the market themselves? Only time will tell with this one, however, given their history of opposing marijuana, we may well see this in the near future.

The other option is that big tobacco will look to diversify its own interests with investments in marijuana firms. For example, Imperial Brands (formerly known as Imperial Tobacco), one of the largest tobacco corporations, recently added Simon Langelier to its board of directors. Langelier is the chairman of PharmaCielo, a Canadian based manufacturer of cannabis oil extracts and other marijuana based health products. The tobacco industry in the US is declining around 4% year on year, and the companies may look to marijuana to help offset some of these expected drops in revenue. We have already seen of these companies diversify into the growing e-cigarette industry, and it is likely that we will see some small scale ventures into the marijuana market within the next 18-24 months. Whether this will result in direct takeover bids for marijuana firms is unknown, but it's something we can't count out at this stage.

Big Pharma vs. The Marijuana Industry

Legal marijuana's biggest enemy, in terms of a specific industry, is the pharmaceutical industry. Big Pharma has a long documented history of opposing any form of marijuana legalization, especially for companies focusing on the medical benefits of marijuana.

In 2016, a $500,000 donation was made to an organization opposing Arizona's recreational marijuana initiative. Donations of $500,000 to major political candidates are not uncommon at all, but ones of this size to a group fighting a signal issue are very rare. That $500,000 came from Insys Therapeutics, who manufacture Subsys, a powerful and extremely addictive Fentanyl based painkiller, targeted at cancer patients. This donation ended up playing a key part, as Arizona's initiative was defeated by the narrow margin of 51-49.

What makes this even more interesting is that Insys is now developing its own line of synthetic THC based drugs. So to make this abundantly clear, this pharmaceutical company not only donated money to help block legalization of recreational marijuana, it then released its own synthetic alternative. It should be noted that in December 2016, former CEO Michael Babich and six more Insys executives were arrested in an alleged bribery case revolving around pressuring doctors to prescribe Subsys, along with defrauding insurance providers. This was done with the motivation of promoting Subsys as an alternative to traditional painkillers and to try to capture market share.

Then you have the case of the 2014 Community Anti Drug Coalition of America (CADCA), where speakers pleaded against the legalization of marijuana. One of the main sponsors of this program was Purdue Pharma, the company that happens to manufacture Oxycontin. Over 1,000 deaths per year in the United States result from overdoses from prescribed Oxycontin. This number soars to over 100,000 when we account for a worldwide scale. Abbott Laboratories, the maker of Vicodin, is another large contributor to CADCA. It is estimated that Big Pharma spends upwards of $20 million per year in lobbying anti-marijuana initiatives.

Early estimates have put medical marijuana's competition as having the ability to cost Big Pharma between $4 and 6 billion per year in direct loss of sales. Washington, for example, has seen a decrease in Medicare prescriptions since the legalization of medical marijuana. Phizer, one of the largest drug companies on the planet as produced data showing that medical marijuana could take as much as $500 million out of its bottom line revenue.

Where Big Pharma's motivations lie to clear to see, the issue is a financial one, rather than a moral one. They are fully aware that nationwide legalization would eat into their market share, as customers seek alternatives to mass manufactured chemical drugs. This competition would lead to lower prices, which is the last thing the pharmaceutical industry is interested in.

Therefore it is likely we will be seeing more companies follow the lead on Insys, in manufacturing their own synthetic THC and CBD based drugs, which could bypass federal restrictions and therefore be sold in regular pharmacies across the country, rather than only in specialist cannabis stores. The potential market size for this is huge, as it is now estimated that over 100 million Americans now depends on some form of painkiller on a daily basis. This includes both doctor prescribed medications such as Vicodin or Percocet, as well as street drugs like Heroin. One thing marijuana enthusiasts have long since spoken out against is the possibility that Big Pharma could use its own pockets to corner the market with these synthetic cannabis drugs, as the general population will view them as "safer" due to their presence in regular pharmacies.

It will be interesting to monitor drug developments in the next 18-24 months from this larger pharmaceutical companies, as they seek to get their own share of the ever growing medical marijuana market. I would predict that we will be seeing more and more synthetic cannabis based drug options emerging from the traditional pharmaceutical companies.

Cannabinoids

You may have seen reports of companies who are focused on "cannabis medicine", what these companies do is utilize cannabinoids to create drugs and formulas to treat various diseases.

For those are you who aren't familiar, cannabinoids are the chemical compounds found in the marijuana plant itself. The main ones being THC, the psychoactive compound, which creates the "high" marijuana is known for. The other main compound is CBD, unlike THC, CBD is non-psychoactive, so you can take pure CBD based products and not feel a "high". Because of this distinction, CBD is legal in more states. There are also other compounds such as CBN, CBG and CBC.

There are a number of biotech companies which focus more on the cannabinoid side of things, by developing pharmaceuticals using these compounds as a major or periphery ingredient. The growth of stocks like these is largely dependent on FDA approval for their drugs, and if you've been in biotech for a while, you'll know this is a slow process.

One of the largest players in this market is the UK based GW Pharmaceuticals. Their main cannabis related product is Sativex. A spray that can help alleviate the symptoms of Multiple Sclerosis. Currently, Sativex has regulatory approval in 16 markets, with 12 more pending. Another drug, Epidiolex, aimed at treating child-onset epilepsy is currently in the pending approval stage as well.

Other significant players in the cannabinoid markets are MedReleaf, Tilray and OrganiGram, all three of these companies are based in Canada are produce CBD based drugs which aid treatment of various health ailments. We'll discuss both MedReleaf and OrganiGram in greater depth later on in this book, as both companies have some very exciting prospects up their sleeves.

"Non-Marijuana" Marijuana Stocks

There are a number of companies that you may well be aware of, and may even hold in your portfolio already, which actually have significant ties to the marijuana industry. As such, I have dubbed these "non-marijuana" marijuana stocks due to their primary business being in different industries.

One such example of this is Scott's Miracle-Gro. A long-time leader in the traditional home and garden care market, a market that usually produces slow, steady, unspectacular returns. Scott's has been a long-time favourite among many US households and known for their TV commercials.

However what you may not have known about Scott's is that 11% of their sales are now derived from a subsidiary company, Hawthorne Gardening Co. Hawthrone focuses its efforts on the medical marijuana industry, and has been steadily acquiring smaller marijuana businesses over the past few years. There additional focus of the business is on the technological side of things, mainly in Hydroponics, which is the act of growing plants in water enriched with minerals and nutrients. In 2017, Hawthorne's sales tripled, and those numbers are projected to continue rising as we move forward.

Even if sentiment completely reverses regarding marijuana and legalization, Scott's can still fall back on its bread and butter business of traditional lawn care, which makes up 89% of the business in total.

The other issue we can look at is the potential for Big Pharma companies to try to acquire some of these cannabis producers as a hedge against their own day-to-day business operations. These companies have very deep pockets, especially compared to even the bigger marijuana firms. We may see some of the pharmaceutical giants make takeover plays for cannabinoid based biotech firms in the next few years.

Marijuana Industry & Red Tape

Now here's where the state legalization vs. Federal legalization issue gets hairy. Because banks have to comply with federal laws regarding issues like money laundering, this directly affects the day to day marijuana business. You see, as a result of this confusing status, many marijuana businesses have zero access to credit. Some can barely get access to more than a basic checking account. This is because it is entirely possible for a bank to be charged with money laundering if they deal with marijuana businesses. Although I should note at this time, there have been zero instances of this. At the time of writing it is estimated that one third of licensed marijuana vendors have been denied a bank account. There are also no tax breaks for marijuana businesses. In a similar law that was aimed at preventing illegal drug dealers from deducting business expenses, marijuana companies are now feeling the effects. A strange caveat to this is that businesses such as prostitution and contract killing can still claim deductions. I know what you're thinking, and you are correct hitmen can claim business expenses. The ramifications for this are large across the industry, basic business expenses such as rent, advertising, wages and utilities (a big one for the growers) are not allowed to be claimed by owners of marijuana businesses.

Where this hits home on the bottom line is that many marijuana businesses are looking at effective tax rates (the percentage of their *pre-tax* profits) of 70%, as opposed to the much lower 30% for other businesses. In terms of the larger conglomerates, it is estimated that many US businesses pay an effective rate as low as 12.5%. What's worse is that marijuana businesses can be on the hook for federal tax evasion if they don't comply with these laws. We should remember that it was a federal tax evasion charge that ended up bringing down Al Capone's entire empire in the 1930s.

There is hope though, in 2017, a bi-partisan act introduced by Senator Ron Wyden and Senator Rand Paul would allow marijuana businesses to make the standard business tax deductions. However, the bill is currently stuck in committee though, and it may well be years before it is able to be passed and enacted.

What's more is, many of these businesses are forced to operate in cash. This gets even more absurd when you consider that even though marijuana is still illegal at a federal level, due to tax code 280E, which requires drug dealers to report their illicit profits for tax purposes, the IRS collects roughly $3 billion per year from marijuana vendors. This leads to a number of stories where marijuana vendors are having to pay the IRS in cash at their local office. Marijuana is certainly beneficial to the IRS and industry growth would lead to even more revenue down the line. Data shows that legal marijuana could lead a 6 fold increase in federal tax revenue.

Why could this all go wrong?

All investments come with a certain amount of risk, and it's always good to analyze the contrarian view of the situation, so we will do so here. Here are a number of factors that could mean this all ends in disappointment. I should note before we begin this section, that this is all speculation. Thus you should take it with a pinch of salt.

Industry Consolidation

The astounding growth rate for the industry thus far, and the continued predictions of 26% per year for the next 3 years. However this does mean we're yet to see any sort of industry consolidation, many of these smaller companies especially will be absorbed into the larger marijuana conglomerates that will no doubt be formed within the next few years.

On the flipside of this though, investing early in these smaller companies could well lead to big gains if they are bought out, rather than run out of business by these larger firms.

Penny stocks

Many of these smaller marijuana stocks are defined as penny stocks as they trade under $5/share. Therefore they can't be listed on the NASDAQ or New York Stock Exchange. Many of them will list on Over The Counter (OTC) exchanges, which have lower requirements and monitoring standards than the bigger exchanges you'll be more familiar with.

This makes them more liable to misinformation and less than stellar business practices. I would exercise caution to these tiny marijuana based stocks, as like other penny stocks, they are more likely to be manipulated than larger ones.

News flows slower in the OTC world as well, so investors looking for up to date information regarding important metrics like cash flow, may well be left in the dark for a longer period than they are comfortable with.

The other factor is the vast majority of penny stocks are companies with less than solid fundamentals in the first place. Most penny stock companies are losing money every year, which is a big part of their low price. Others do not yet have a working product and are banking on future approval in order to their stock increase price.

When researching these stocks, you will see phrases like "expansion phase" "potential revenue" and "impressive management team" rather than talk of consistent profitability or market share.

There will also be a group of people shilling the stock on message boards or in private Discord groups. You'll see phrases like "get on the train", "10X by the end of the month" and other fear of missing out type language. If you've been involved with cryptocurrency at all, you'll see the same patterns and language associated with that market.

Like any penny stock, these microcap marijuana companies should be looked at as a speculative gamble, rather than a long or even short term investment. If we want to look at some historical precedence, let's take a look at 6 nanotechnology companies that were previously listed on OTC market. Nanotechnology was another big boom industry in the mid 2000s, and many investors made speculative plays.

JMAR ($JMAR): Down 100% from its peak

Biophan ($BIPH): -99% from its peak

US Global Nanospace ($USGA): -99% from its peak

Industrial Nanotech ($INTK): -96% from its peak

Natural Nano ($NNAN): -99% from its peak

mPhase ($XDSL): Down -99% from its peak

If you had invested $1,000 in each of these companies, so $6,000 total, you would currently have **15 cents to show for your initial investment.** So if you are not an experienced investor, or you don't have deep pockets, I would urge you to stay well away from these microcap companies for the reasons listed above.

Jeff Sessions

Attorney General Sessions is one of the biggest critics of the marijuana industry. Sessions has been previously quoted as saying "good people don't smoke marijuana" and "My best view is that we don't need to be legalizing marijuana." Needless to say, statements like these don't fill the room with confidence when it comes to the issue of nationwide legalization.

Sessions also strongly believes the gateway drug theory, that many opioid addicts were exposed to the ideas of illegal drugs via marijuana and thus marijuana is the direct cause of their addictions. Despite a large number of academic studies that have long since refuted this theory, Sessions continues to stand by his views.

What is more concerning is that these statements were made, despite increasing amounts of data supporting the medical and social benefits of legalized marijuana. For example, in 2015 there were 20,101 deaths resulting from opioid related overdoses. Contrast this to a grand total of ZERO deaths from marijuana related overdoses. You can't really argue for stronger data than that when it comes to legalization, and yet here is one of the most powerful men in the country using phrases like "historic drug epidemic".

The positive of this is in the form of the President Donald Trump himself. During his campaign, he stated multiple times that he was a supporter of medical marijuana, and said the issue should be decided at the state level. Trump's views on drug legalization are well documented in the past, and he was even quoted in a 1990 Miami Herald interview as stating "We're losing badly the War on Drugs. You have to legalize drugs to win that war. You have to take the profit away from these drug czars."

However, there is a possibility that Sessions could try to override this by repealing the Rohrabacher-Farrr Amendment. Needless to say, the man who said "I reject the idea that America will be a better place if marijuana is sold in every corner store." is going to be one of the largest hurdles to overcome.

Canada backtracking on legalization

For the Canadian stocks talked about in this book, the path appears to be smoother, but that doesn't mean bumps in the road can't happen. Whilst recreational marijuana legalization is scheduled for summer 2018, a lot can happen between now and then. Originally supports had hoped for an announcement for July 1 2018, which happens to be Canada Day, but Prime Minister Trudeau ruled that out in December 2017. Any further delays could lead to decreased industry confidence, which will no doubt have a negative effect on market sentiment and share prices of Canadian based stocks.

Public Sentiment Regarding Legal Marijuana

The sentiment is an overlooked part of analyzing a market. General public opinion is a huge factor in both the short and long-term growth of an industry. Often, short-term price changes are decided mostly on sentiment rather than any fundamental changes with a company or industry. We have seen this multiple times with cryptocurrency and the price volatility associated with that particular industry.

In February 2018, Marijuana Business Daily released their "Marijuana Business Factbook", an almanac of statistics relating to the marijuana industry and its potential growth going forward. The big takeaway is that they have now upgraded their projection from 3x growth to 4x growth by 2021.

The second biggest indicator that we could be poised for solid long-term gains is the public opinion poll carried out in the research. 59% of Americans now favor legalizing marijuana, a number that continues to creep up every year. In addition to this, only 32% of Americans are now fundamentally *opposed* to legal marijuana. Once again, going by age, the younger generation is more fervent in their support.

In total, there have been 5 major opinion polls in the past year alone, and their results all say the exact same thing. The majority of the US population is in favor of legalization, both on a medical and recreational level. One survey, by Quinnipac, solely focused on medical marijuana, and a whopping 94% of respondents supported the idea.

An Analysis of 12 Marijuana Stocks

In this section we take a look at a number of marijuana stocks, the companies behind them, and how they plan to capture their part of the marijuana market. Not all of these are pure play stocks, so not all of their revenue is directly tied to marijuana, but all of worth investigating, to say the least. As always, I am not recommending you buy any of the stocks listed here.

It should be noted that although a number of these are Canadian stocks, some do trade on OTC exchanges in the United States.

Scotts Miracle-Gro ($SMG)

Price at time of writing: $89.13

Probably the most well known of the "marijuana stocks" in this list. We should note off the bat that the marijuana component only makes up around 10% of Scotts total business, but this is an ever growing proportion. We previously mentioned the 2015 purchase of General Hydroponics, which will be a key factor in Scotts expansion into the marijuana sector going forward. General Hydroponics provides both consumer and industry indoor growing solutions, which will be huge if recreational marijuana is legalized on a wider business, and could result in a rise in the company's important to Scotts bottom line..

A dip in price at the beginning of 2018 was to be expected, as the lawncare business that makes up 90% of Scotts revenue is extremely seasonal. As the hydroponic portion of the business grows this will likely even out as the nature of hydroponics make it a seasonproof growing tool. Grow wise, further expansion into other aspects of the marijuana business may well be on the cards, and a company like Scotts has deeper pockets than most, thus would be able to afford any short term losses as a result of growing pains that these new ventures can often cause.

Another area of interest for long term investors would be Scotts extremely strong fundamentals and track record within the sector. The company is now 150 years old and has been a household name for many years before legalized marijuana was on the radar of most Americans.

GW Pharmaceuticals

Price at time of writing: $126.06

The biotech giant from Britain is one of the more well known "marijuana stocks" although unlike many of the others here, they do not participate in the growing or distribution market. GW's usage of marijuana is in the manufacturing of drugs known as cannabinoids, in which marijuana is a key component.

Their current flagship product is Sativex, the first cannabis based treatment to receive FDA approval in the United States. Sativex helps treat the symptoms of Multiple Sclerosis (MS) including pain relief, bladder control and involuntary muscle spasms. The success of Sativex has helped GW rise into the ranks of one of the top performing biotech stocks of the last few years.

GW is now betting big on Epidiolex, a CBD based drug that will help epilepsy sufferers, particular those with child onset epilepsy. In discussions with insurance providers, it is planned that if approval is gained, the drug will be available to over 200 million Americans on their healthcare plans. As previously discussed, developing new drugs can take a long time when you factor in everything from lab development, multiple testing phrases and the huge amount of red tape that comes with trying to get FDA approval.

GW received good news though in December 2017 when they revealed that the FDA had approved their New Drug Application for Epidiolex. This doesn't mean they have the all clear to manufacture and sell the drug yet, but it is certainly a step in the right direction. If the FDA approves the drug in the middle of 2018, the timeline will mean that the drug could be on the market within 3 months.

There is another cannabinoid in GW's pipeline as well, the lesser reported Cannabidivarin (CBDV) which is being developed to help treat epilepsy in adults. There have already been tested on CBDV in treating symptoms of autism in young children. However the development is in the early stages and therefore will have no bottom line impact on GW's revenue this year, and approval by the end of next year is also unlikely.

GW's strong fundamentals have led to some financial analysts labeling it "the most secure marijuana stock". Whilst biotech as an industry operates different to pure marijuana stocks, there may be additional benefits as any federal rulings on recreational marijuana use are unlikely to affect the development of cannabinoid based drugs. Overall, compared to some of the riskier plays here, GW offers the conservative investor an easy entry point into the marijuana market.

Kush Bottles ($KSHB)

Price at time of writing: $5.50

Kush Bottles is a marijuana company, that doesn't actually deal with the growing or handling of the plant at all. The California firm provides and distributes the materials needed to grow marijuana and marijuana products at an industrial level. This includes everything from child-safe packaging, labels, vape pens, cannabis pipes and other paraphernalia. Their flagship product is a plastic tube to safely store a pre-rolled marijuana joint. While this may seem fairly inconsequential, pre-rolled joints are a big feature of legal marijuana that did not exist when it was still illegal. Every marijuana dispensary worth its salt features pre-rolled joints heavily, and being able to capture this part of the market could mean big things for Kush Bottles going forward. Currently, the firm boasts over 4,000 legal marijuana customers, and in a sales presentation July, stated they sold over 1 million of their pre-rolled tubes to dispensaries every month.

The company is still very much in its early stages, with only $18.8 million in recorded revenue in 2017. However, the firm is not up to it neck in debt like many smaller marijuana companies which can be seen as a big positive. In its first 3 years of business, the firm has acquired 3 competitors already in the form of Dank Bottles, CMP Wellness and Roll-Uh-Bowl.

Growing pains will be in line with many other marijuana firms regarding basics like tax deductions and banking regulations.

Cronos Group ($MJN)

Price at time of writing: $9.20CAD

Cronos Group takes a slightly different approach to the industry. Rather than focusing its effects on cultivation or distribution of marijuana, the firm acts as an investment group for Canadian medical marijuana companies. The firm currently owns 3 marijuana companies outright and has partial holdings in 3 more.

Cronos is betting big on the proposed legalization in summer 2018. Legalization would give a boost to all of its companies, and the diversified nature of its investment mean it can withstand additional competition in certain parts of the industry such as growing. Competition is still a concern industry-wide, and short-term effects could be an increase in advertising spend as it fights for market position. However, this should not be a concern for those looking to hold long-term.

Another thing to note is that Cronos and its subsidiaries are not yet profitable, so investors can expect additional share issuances. The amount of shares in play has increased by a factor of 10 within the last 4 years, and with each new issuance comes a devaluing in the current value of shares. In terms of short-term viability, Cronos has a lot of eggs in the legalization basket, so it may be worth holding off on pulling the trigger until that matter is sorted out.

Emerald Health Therapeutics ($EMH)

Price at time of writing: $6.53 CAD

The Canadian pharmaceuticals company, formerly known as T-Bird Health Inc. is another company with more of a focus on the medical marijuana space. The company producers cannabis oils, dried cannabis as well as marijuana based health solutions in capsule form.

The firm is more research based than other medical cannabis producers and makes an effort to identify the most important qualities in each marijuana strain, before isolating those properties and creating new products from them.

Growth towards the end of 2017 was fueled by a purchase of additional growing space and the company was also given a recent upgrade to Tier 1 by the Toronto Stock Exchange. This indicates solid financial reporting practices and generally shows the company is well run.

One additional point of interest with EMH is their adoption of blockchain technology. Blockchain technology is the underlying digital ledger which allows cryptocurrency to function securely among other things. EMH will be using the technology to help develop supply chain and ecommerce solutions in a joint venture with DMG Blockchain Solutions. The venture will be named CannaChain Technologies and as expected, will focus its initial efforts on the legal cannabis industry.

Medical Marijuana Inc. ($MJNA)

Price at time of writing: $0.11

Famous for being the first publicly traded marijuana company in the United States. The stock has been trading for over 4 years, which makes it a grandfather in a space seeing new firms pop up every week. The firm operates in both the marijuana and industrial hemp fields. This includes selling hemp oil, CBD oil and other cannabinoids aiming to treat various health ailments.

Because none of these oils are THC based, MJNA operates more on the legal side of things than other companies. CBD oil, for example, is legal in all 50 states. However, recent FDA rulings may complicate this matter, as the FDA wishes to regulate CBD based products due to them containing miniscule amounts of THC. This continued fight led to share prices tumbling more than 70% in 2017, and there doesn't seem to be much potential good news on the horizon for the company.

The company operates a number of subsidiaries, which has led to small calling it a small scale marijuana ETF. The interesting structure of these companies and exactly how their profitability works is a factor that could lead to investor caution. There is also their large numbers of shares issued (3 billion at time of writing) which may also be a factor in looking elsewhere for solid marijuana investments. As such, MJNA looks at this stage to be a highly speculative play at best, and one probably suited more towards serious investors with much experience in penny stocks.

MedReleaf ($MEDFF)

Price at time of writing: $18.00 CAD

MedReleaf is another Canadian company just spends more of its focus on the medical marijuana side of things. As a manufacturer and producer of cannabis oils and dried cannabis, it targets those holding medical marijuana cards. Their 2017 IPO was North America's largest marijuana IPO yet.

The medical marijuana industry in Canada continues to grow at a rate of 10% per month, that's right, not per year but per month. Cannabis oils are growing even faster than that at a rate of around 16% per month. Oils have a much higher margin than dried cannabis, and therefore MedReleaf is able to grow its earnings at a much higher rate than competitor companies who only focus on the dried plant. The company controls roughly 45% of the cannabis oil market in the country, and with their expanded production facility, this percentage could well go even higher.

This has led the company to post decent financial numbers in the past few years. Although the company is not yet as profitable as others like Canopy and Aphria, it continues to be well run and has not yet diluted shares to raise capital like some of its competitors.

MedReleaf's growth plans include expanding their Bradford production facility to 86,000 square feet. This will allow the company to keep up with the ever increasing demand, especially if the legalized recreational marijuana bill passes this year. Their focus on higher margin products, and positioning to take advantage of any proposed legalization makes MedReleaf a very exciting prospect to watch. Most marijuana companies aren't profitable and are betting on the future rather than the present. MedReleaf is one of the rare exceptions to this rule.

Organigram Holdings ($OGRMF)

Price at time of writing: $3.30

Based in New Brunswick, Organigram is one of only two companies (the other being marijuana giant Canopy Growth) with a license to produce marijuana in the province. Why this is important, is that New Brunswick is the only Canadian province with fully legal recreational marijuana use. This led to an almost 200% increase in the number of patients that Organigram serves, with this total projected to rise further in the next 12 months. All of this comes before nationwide legalization currently scheduled for summer 2018.

With estimated produce levels topping 65,000 kilograms a year, the firm shows that it means business. All this comes from just a single production facility, which Organigram plans to expand in 2018. As well as moving into higher margin strains of marijuana. The company also has a dried cannabis sales arm, although the growth of that element of the business has been slow.

This makes Organigram a prime target for a buyout from one of the larger corporations. With a market cap of $400 million, along with its previous connections and licenses, one of the bigger firms may well be taking a look at Organigram as a way to enter New Brunswick. The company also has an agreement in place to supply Prince Edward Island with 1 million grams a year which will work out in an additional $7-9 million in sales.

Potential problems include the ability to scale their operations that quickly, especially when marijuana companies are in somewhat of an arms race to increase their production yield as fast as possible. Being first to market when the recreational legalization deal is made will be huge, and Organigram is competing against some heavy hitters in this respect. Their current agreements alone though make them well worth checking out.

Update: A February press release noted that OrganiGram had received additional licenses to expand their production facilities. Construction of a new facility with estimated 65,000 kilogram yield per year is now due to begin in April 2018. This is very positive news for the company going forward.

Canopy Growth Corp ($TWNJF)

Price at time of writing: $22.35

Canada's Canopy Growth Corp is a big player which currently holds around a 20% market share.

Canopy has been quick to expand, and last year purchased Mettrum Health in a deal which included 2.4 million square feet of land with the capacity for growing marijuana.

Obviously, the big external factor will be whether Canada passes legal recreational marijuana in the summer of 2018 as is expected. Currently, there don't seem to be too many hurdles in the way, and Prime Minister Justin Trudeau is leading the charge himself. One important factor to note is that the proposed tax rate for the newly legalized marijuana is much lower than any of the state tax rates we have seen in the United States so far. This will allow marijuana to be priced at more competitive rates, and eliminate competition from the black market, which has been a thorn in the side of some states like Washington.

This is combined with the number of Canadian medical marijuana increasing by a staggering rate of almost 10% per month. Canopy's Canadian presence is one of the factors that helped it overtake GW Pharmaceuticals as the world's largest marijuana stock by market cap in November 2017.

Canopy also exports dried marijuana to many European countries that have legalized the drug including the Netherlands.

One factor to watch with Canopy is if the new legislation brings about an influx of competition in the space. While this is to be expected, it remains to be seen what effect this will have on Canopy stock prices going forward. Needless to say though, for the time being, Canopy can safely say it holds the position as King of the Legal Marijuana industry.

General Cannabis Corp ($CANN)

Price at time of writing: $4.12

General Cannabis Corp has a wide range of business including consulting, advisory, marketing, and management services to the marijuana industry. Their holdings include a 3 acre property in Colorado, as well as a branding and marketing firm that targets the marijuana industry.

Their website doesn't really tell you more than that, using terms like "trusted partner" and "turn your dreams into reality." rather than making more concrete statements about what the company can do for potential clients. The homepage also features a stock ticker, and the company Instagram account, which are two facets of business that don't usually appear side by side.

The balance sheets are rather alarming with less than $300,000 in assets and over $4.5 million in liabilities. That ratio alone is frankly terrifying. The company also made a $9 million loss in the past year with just $2 million in gross sales. With numbers like this, it's hard to say just how much of a future the company has, and it obviously cannot continue to make big losses like this. Overall, I can't see much upside for General Cannabis Corp and its investors going forward.

Aphria ($APH)

Price at time of writing: $16.08CAD

Aphria concentrates on providing hydroponic solutions for medical marijuana. The company currently has a partnership with the Canadian government and this is part of the reason the stock tripled in price during 2017. The company currently has around 40,000 patients and a fledgling nationwide distribution system.

Aphria is one stock that defies industry norms in terms of producing positive revenue growth and ending the financial year in the black. Strong fundamentals like this make the stock a promising one to monitor as we go forward. Revenue increased by 62% last year and the last quarter's earnings were also positive. The ability to not only promise a product, but actually deliver on a profitable one, is something that could well indicate strong long term potential.

The company also acquired Broken Coast Cannabis for $230 million (note: this was a largely stock funded deal with only a small fraction coming in cash), which gives them better access to Canada's West Coast. Late January also brought news of the acquisition of Nuuvera in a huge $826 million cash and stock deal. The deal was made with the intention of moving growth beyond the Canadian borders, and international expansion seems to be on the cards. Nuuvera was already working with parties in Germany, Israel and Italy to explore distribution opportunities for newly legalized medical marijuana. The Italian market alone is worth around $9 billion annually and Nuuvera is one of the few foreign companies with a license to export goods to Italy. This aggressive growth strategy is one that may put Aphria into the big leagues in an industry that is consolidating at rapid rates.

February brought news of an international supply chain agreement with Cannabis Wheaton. This will help both companies advance their distribution strategies in order to keep up with the ever increasing demand. This may be bigger news for Wheaton than Aphria in the short term due to the company's smaller size, but working agreements like this show that co-operation on future projects, which may have more benefit to Aphria, is on the cards.

Corbus Pharmaceuticals ($CRBP)

Price at time of writing: $7.05

Corbus is focused strictly on the medical side of the marijuana equation. It's currently betting big on its drug Anabasum. Anabasum aims to treat sclerosis and has done well in initial trials. There are also plans to trial the same drug in relation to Lupus.

After a meteoric rise at the beginning of 2017, with prices soaring over 500% in the first 3 months, the stock began to cool off towards the end of the year. Like most smaller cap companies, Corbus is yet to be profitable. Current cash flow analysis indicates the company has enough money to continue its day-to-day operations into Q4 2019. Although this could be extended with a stock offering.

The obvious concern is whether Corbus is a one trick pony, and as of right now, that's probably a correct assumption to make. If Anabasum doesn't get approved then its back to square one, and with a lack of profitability, that may well be it for Corbus. However, if Anabasum continues to produce positive results and ends up getting FDA approval, then Corbus will move on to bigger and better things, much to the delight of investors.

Marijuana ETFs

At the time of writing, there are 3 approved marijuana ETFs in North America, with two more scheduled for launch in February 2018. For those of you looking for a more low-risk, hands off option for investing in marijuana stocks, one of these ETFs may be exactly what you are looking for. That's before the obvious advantages of ETFs like only paying 1 commission vs. Upwards of 15 commissions if you were to buy the individual stocks.

In December 2017, ETFMG Alternative Harvest ETF became the first ETF to list on a US stock exchange. We have previously mentioned this ETF and discussed how their decision to pivot from Latin American real estate to the marijuana industry may be cause for concern. The move comes with buying popular marijuana stocks such as Canopy, Aurora and GW Pharma.

The price action after the move was heavily in the positive direction, just take a look at this chart from Bloomberg after the decision to buy marijuana stocks occurred.

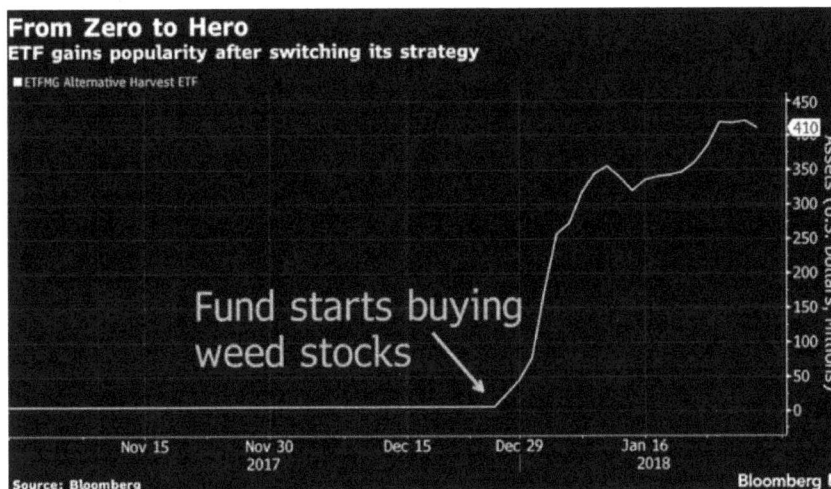

From Zero to Hero
ETF gains popularity after switching its strategy
■ ETFMG Alternative Harvest ETF

Fund starts buying weed stocks

Source: Bloomberg   Bloomberg

What you may not know about this ETF that's been in the news so much over the past 2 months is that it's Custodian Bancorp is considering dropping the ETF due to its drastic switch in the business model. This move also appears to be based on the uncertain future of federal level marijuana legalization. There is, of course, the probability that if Bancorp does drop the ETF, that another bank will step in and fill its shoes. However, if they cannot find a replacement, the ETF will have to be liquidated.

Switching focus is not necessarily uncommon for an investment group to do, however, it is the complete industry pivot that is something we must examine. As indicated by the graph above, the fund remained relatively flat before the move to marijuana, so their track record in other industries isn't something we can verify. The next 6 months will be interesting and it remains to be seen if they can replicate their initial short term success.

Horizons Marijuana Life Sciences ETF ($HMMJ)

Price at time of writing: $18.76CAD

Launched on the Toronto Stock Exchange in April 2017, this ETF has been one of the top performers since the beginning. Posting gains of over 85% in 2017, although it has experienced some pullback to start 2018.

The fund focuses more on the medical marijuana industry and has a policy of not buying any companies that focus strictly on recreational marijuana in the US or Canada. However, this view is likely to change depending on how quickly legalization occurs in both countries. You can certainly expect investments in recreational marijuana companies if legalization goes through in Canada this year as expected.

The fund holds 30 stocks, which is generally considered a low number for an ETF, and as such your diversification is lower than other ETFs, making it naturally a riskier proposition. Another factor to examine is the proportion of the fund that is held in the top 20 stocks. In the case of HMMJ, the top 10 (not 20) stocks make up over 80% of the fund, which is somewhat concerning for the low-risk investor. The top 4 holdings are naturally the large Canadian medical marijuana companies, namely Canopy Growth Corp, Aurora Cannabis, Aphria and MedReleaf.

Some investors would like to see additional diversification in form of biotech companies and cannabinoid firms, although these companies tend to be in the slower growth rate sphere due to the long process of their drugs receiving approval, and therefore aren't without risk themselves.

HMMJ is certainly the most fundamentally sound marijuana ETF, and with a management fee of 0.75% plus sales tax, it's not an expensive one for the retail investor to get involved with either. If you are looking for a lower-risk way to enter the marijuana market, this could well be it.

Horizon Marijuana Growers ETF ($HMJR)

Price at time of writing: Not yet launched

Another ETF by Horizon, this one focuses on the growing and cultivation part of the industry in particular. This particular ETF consist mainly of small cap companies with upside potential and aims to take advantage of increased demand for marijuana across Canada pending the legalization of recreational marijuana.

One interesting thing to note about this ETF is that 20% of the holdings will be made up of overseas companies, in the first instance, this will be growers from Australia. This could certainly help negate some of the risks that comes with banking on summer 2018 Canadian legalization. The first group of holdings has CANN Group as the largest with 7.24% with its Australian growing company AusCANN making up a slightly lower portion of the fund.

The fund will have a 0.85% management fee. So if you're someone who has huge faith in the demand for growers, then this ETF might be a smart play for a low-risk investor who doesn't want to go in on just one or two individual companies.

Evolve Marijuana ETF ($SEED)

Price at time of writing: Not yet launched

Scheduled for Launch on February 12th 2018, this will be the 4th ETF in North America and will trade on the Toronto Stock Exchange. Evolve Funds Group CEO Raj Lala stated the fund aims to take advantage of "a 60-per-cent compounded annual growth rate in the next few years." It is unclear just which sector of the market the ETF will target, but they have stated they will be investing in both domestic and global marijuana companies. The initial focus will be on the Canadian market, but as legalization gets more traction worldwide, expansion beyond its borders will occur. You can fully expect that the big Canadian companies like Aurora, Canopy and Cronos Group will be among the initial portfolio of holdings. It has also been stated that the fund will have a management fee of 0.75% per year. Evolve has a strong track record and their first venture into the marijuana market will be an interesting one to monitor. Another Marijuana ETF, run by Redwood Investments is due to launch around the same time period.

Can non-Canadian residents buy Canadian stocks?

As you may have seen, a large number of these stocks are listed on the Toronto Stock Exchange, Canada's largest stock exchange. Some are also listed on US regulated exchanges, which means you can buy them using a local broker, or broker who supports US stocks if you are based outside of the US.

You can also buy Canadian stocks from many online brokers including TD Ameritrade, Schwab and E-Trade, however, there may be higher commissions than US stocks when using these sites. Some of the commissions can be as high as $19 per trade. I advise you to check your broker's rates for Canadian stocks, and it may be easier to call them on the phone than dig through the website looking for rates. At the time of writing, only Schwab uses the same rates for both US and Canadian stocks.

It should be noted that some online brokers do not directly buy Canadian stocks, they instead purchase pink sheets as a proxy for the stock. These pink sheets will have a 1:1 value, but trading volume will be lower than the volume on Canadian exchanges. So this is something to look out for if you are planning on buying or selling large amounts, and I would recommend double checking with your broker before executing any trades. The other thing to note is if you are using a US broker, you may be looking for a different stock symbol than the ones listed in this book. These symbols will usually be 5 letters long, so make sure to check your particular stock's corresponding US symbol before you accidentally buy shares of the wrong company.

Should I still invest in Marijuana Stocks if I'm fundamentally against marijuana as a drug?

Obviously, some more socially conservative investors will have an opposition to marijuana stocks. Many of these companies will fall into the same category of "sin stocks" as alcohol and tobacco companies, and if you are morally opposed to investing your money in these kinds of companies, that's OK.

On top of that, as we have previously discussed, marijuana still remains illegal at a federal level, and there are a number of ramifications that come alongside this decision. It should be noted, that obviously any publicly traded marijuana stock is conducting its business within the eyes of the law, this goes for small cap stocks traded on OTC exchanges as well as larger cap ones on the NYSE or the Toronto Stock Exchange.

However, that doesn't mean you have to miss out on one of the hottest asset classes in the past 10 years. There are still a number of companies that are focused more on the beneficial side of marijuana. These would be companies more on the biotech side of things that are focused on utilizing marijuana and components like CBD, to cure help diseases.

Firms such as GW Pharmaceuticals fit this bill well, with their epilepsy drug Epidiolex. We should reiterate at this point that CBD, unlike THC, does not have any capacity to alter one's mindstate, so users will not experience a regular marijuana "high". There is also InSys Pharmaceuticals, who we have discussed previously, and their subsidiary company SubSys which is developing a drug called Syndros to assist in helping weight loss associated with chemotherapy.

Other companies like Scotts Miracle Gro have a small marijuana element to their business and as such, can be solid plays without needing to tell your friends you bought a "pot stock". These are just a few options if you wish to get a part of the pie, without committing yourself to a pure marijuana stock and going against your own individual moral code.

Conclusion

Well there we have it, an introduction to the exciting world of marijuana stocks, and the potential benefits of investing in them. Like I said before, this market is projected to triple in size in the next 3 years, and there is enormous opportunity across many factors of the industry. From growing to manufacturing and distribution and real estate, marijuana is going to make a lot of people rich in the few years. Like any industry, there is risk involved, and I urge you to do additional research on top of what you've read in this book. There are also a number of external factors to consider, many of these are out of the control of the companies they will affect, so it would be wise to monitor any legalization news closely. Marijuana is still in the early stages as an asset class, so as such many of these companies should be looked at as more speculative plays, similar to cryptocurrency in this respect. Therefore they should not make up a significant portion of your portfolio. I hope you've enjoyed what you have read in this book, and if you do decide to invest in marijuana stocks, I hope you make a lot of money.

Thanks,

Stephen

Stock Market Investing for Beginners

The Top 101 Growth Stocks for 2019 – Including

Marijuana Stocks, 5G Stocks, Penny Stocks and Dividends

+ How to Build a Starter Portfolio for Less than $100

Written By

Everyman Investing

Introduction

So you want to make a million dollars in the stock market? Is that possible and if it is, how does one accomplish it? Well, to answer both of those questions yes it is possible and there are many ways to accomplish it. For sure, it is easier if you have six figures to invest, but what if you only have five, four, or even three to get the job done? Yes, it can still be done with the right strategy and patience. It does not happen overnight and can take many years of up and down roller coaster riding to accomplish your goals. So you need to be prepared to choose the right stocks, leave your money in them, and watch the market religiously.

I am not talking about becoming a day trader watching a screen all day or someone chained to the stock market scroll, but just being someone that is aware of how trends affect companies and when to move or hold your position based on those. The best strategy is one where you do all of the research and leg work up front and then simply "lock and load" when it comes time to invest. That strategy is to pick the best growth stocks, invest early, and let your money grow with the stock. How do you pick those? By becoming aware of current business trends and growth industries from which the best growth stocks will come.

This book will give you the blueprint to choose from over 100 of them, starting for $100 or less. You will learn their industries, and be aware of how trends may change them in the future. The key to achieving financial freedom is to learn to spot those winners, invest, and hold. So, if you are ready to become a junior analyst and a wise investor, read on.

Chapter One: Growth Stocks

What are Growth Stocks? Well, in short, they are companies that grow higher than the market average. In addition, they do not give out dividends (or payments back to the stockholders for profits and growth each quarter) but instead, invest those back into the business to keep growing. When compared with traditional or Blue Chip stocks that pay those dividends, it can seem like a speculative or risky investment. However, what you must realize is that earnings from the rising stock price are usually more long term and outpace what might have come from a dividend. These stocks are usually tied to the hot growth industries which carry current biotech, marijuana, cloud technology, AI, 5G cellular, and nanotechnology. Their price on the exchange is considered their actual value no matter how high the price and you earn profits from the steady growth of the exchange price over a period of at least five years. Think of the appreciation of the price of a house or luxury car. It is much the same here, all profits are capital gains based on the resale of the stock. Very simple no muss no fuss and no complicated algorithms.

Here are some simple methods for picking Growth Stocks per Stockpicking.com

- Strong historical earnings growth. Companies should show a track record of strong earnings growth over the previous 5 to 10 years. The general idea is that if the company has displayed good growth in the recent past, it's likely to continue doing so moving forward.

- Strong forward earnings growth. Watch out for the release of the company's earnings reports (required by law for public corporations). This is an official public statement of a company's profitability for a specific period – typically a quarter or a year. These announcements are made on specific dates usually according to the quarter system and are linked to estimates that are issued by analysts. If it shows better than average or at least average growth, the stock is a good bet.

- Strong profit margins. A company's profit is calculated by deducting all expenses from sales (barring taxes) and dividing by sales. It's an important metric to consider because a company can have fantastic growth in sales but poor profit margins. This would mean that the upper management is not great at controlling costs in relation to revenues. If a company exceeds its previous five-year average of pretax profit margins – as well as those of its industry – the company may be a good growth candidate.

- Strong return on equity. The return on equity (ROE) measures its profit margin based on the money shareholders have invested. It's calculated by dividing net income by shareholder equity. Stable or increasing ROE indicates that management is doing a good job generating returns from shareholders' investments or money borrowed and is operating the business efficiently.

- Strong stock performance. In general, if a stock cannot realistically double in five years, **it's probably not a growth stock**. Keep in mind, a stock's price would double in seven years with a growth rate of just 10%. To double in five years, the growth rate must be 15%. But really it is much simpler, if you don't see growths of double, don't bother.

Ask a broker, a member of management, or yourself the following:

(Source: investopedia.com)

Question 1: *Where do you see sales trending in the next 12 to 24 months?*

A longer time period will give the investor a good glimpse of the opportunities and the risks that could present themselves over both the short and intermediate-term. Make sure you keep watch on the stock for an extended period.

Question 2: *What are the risks associated with the sourcing of raw material, or holding the line on costs of services?*

By asking this question, you will be able to learn whether there are any potential difficulties for the company in terms of acquiring raw materials or labor in the future. This can give you an idea of how the company's profit may change in the intermediate and long-term.

Question 3: *What is the best use for the cash on the company's balance sheet?*

This question will indicate whether the company is planning a large scale expansion or merger. It will also indicate whether or not they are a conservative type of management or are more interested in how they are perceived. Look for a response that would key in on whether the company is taking steps to improve its place in the market. If the company isn't growing and is losing cash, then you know what kind of performance to expect.

Question 4: *Who are the emerging competitors in the industry in which you operate?*

This question will let indicate whether they know who to watch out for and they're up against. It may also let you know of unknown rivals that may be coming to market, which could impact the company at some point down the road. Consequently, management may also disclose how it plans to deal with its new or existing competitors all together

Question 5: *What part or aspect of the business is giving you the most trouble now?*

The answer will show weaknesses in the company's organization and provide some insight into future earnings. For example, if the manager indicates that one or more sections or divisions were unprofitable or too expensive to operate this will give you a good indication that there is a hole that needs to be plugged. Identifying problem areas is just one part of the equation. It is far more important to hear about solutions to the problem.

Question 6: *How close is Wall Street in terms of estimating your company's earnings results?*

With this question, you're asking if the company will meet or beat the street's estimate. If the manager indicates that they are always under or even overestimated by analysts then it could be an indication that the "street" is off on this company and that could be problematic.

Question 7: *What part of the business do you think is being ignored that has more upside potential than Wall Street is giving it?*

This question will show the managers passion. That could be an indicator that he/she or the entire management team has a positive outlook on the business. If they do not then that is a huge problem in itself. However, if they are overconfident in the face of contrary evidence, this could be a sign that they will run an unsubstantiated "maverick" strategy that in a solid company can be a huge advantage, but in a problem company can lead to ruin.

Question 8: *Do you have any plans to advance or promote the stock?*

Knowing whether management plans to promote the stock to all investors is a sign that either they believe in themselves or they don't. The savvy investor can buy into the stock ahead of what could be a large amount of buying pressure.

Question 9: *What catalysts will affect the stock going forward?*

The manager is likely to give the investor a wealth of information. This is due to the fact people like to talk about both their and their company's accomplishments. Whether or not they speak the facts will let you know what the future outlook will be. Including investment information about negative catalysts that could adversely impact the share price.

Growth Industries

No investment strategy suits every type of person all the time. This is particularly true for young Millennial and Generation Z investors. However, identifying growth stocks and industries is always a wise bet. As such, high-growth stocks are ideal for both young-adult and novice investors. Most young investors have 80% of their portfolio in stocks, and the remainder in safer, interest-yielding assets. Time is money and the extra time allows riskier investments to expand to their full potential. With the Bull Market we are experiencing, now is a perfect chance to take advantage of longer-term growth forecasts.

Whenever discussions about high-growth stocks arise, one must talk about e-commerce and how it overwhelmingly dominates the retail sector. Remember the newer generation has grown up in a time without the brick-and-mortar hegemony and thus is more inclined to participate in the e-commerce sector.

Considering that young people do nearly everything online, e-commerce companies that sell unorthodox items and charge a premium for them are the wave of the future. In addition, the fact that half of the US workforce will be independent contractors by 2020 also means that apps and companies intended to help with that transition will be a huge source of growth. For those of you who have worked in Fortune 500 or 100 companies, you have seen the intensity of big organizations. They need help to handle the needs of tens of thousands of workers and they need unified platforms to help find both employees and contractors.

Another factor is that by the time Millennials are looking at retirement, marijuana will have likely become legal. In fact, rumors are it may be legalized nationwide by 2020. Just as the Prohibition Era failed to curb Americans' desire for alcohol, the current period will fail to reduce people's desire for cannabis. This is in addition to the numerous beneficial uses of its derivatives. It's only a matter of time before the government listens to the will of the people. When that day comes, companies dealing in marijuana such as Cannabis Growth Corporation will exponentially rise in value.

Next, as more people are cashless and paying for things card-free with apps, any payment processor will be a great growth stock.

The world of virtual living and having everything in the home on a "smart system" is the next big thing. So, investing in companies that produce wireless and AI related products is a boon. Experts forecast that by the year 2020, home automation will become a $50 billion industry.

1.Biotech-In layman's terms is the process of combining biological elements with synthetic elements to produce a molecular change and a whole new product or function from the originals. This is what the companies that make up this sector do. The sector is divided into four different categories of companies. Those that make products for healthcare, agriculture/food, industrial (chemicals for cleaning and non-edible function including environmentally friendly products), fuel, land preservation, and warfare. The Biotech Industry is divided into many different subcategories based on the sub-sector they serve:

A. Gold Biotech - these are companies that use computer components and mechanics to affect biological issues-such as pharma and medical technologies for surgery or treatment.

B. Blue Biotech - this centers on the use of sea algae to create new sources of fuel.

C. Green Biotech - these companies focus on agriculture and genetic manipulation of seeds and waste/pest reduction.

D. Red Biotech - companies focusing on genetic engineering for disease prevention like stem cells.

E. White Biotech - focuses on new chemicals or enzymes that can make the manufacturing process cheaper and faster.

F. Yellow Biotech - focuses on food production and new genetic strains of food crops.

G. Gray Biotech - focuses on the preservation of ecological diversity and lowering levels of pollution.

H. Brown Biotech - these companies focus on rehabilitating arid areas like desserts to make them capable of supporting life.

I. Violet Biotech - focuses on using technology to solve social issues.

J. Dark Biotech - focuses on the darker side of Biotech such as chemical and biological weapons.

2.Marijuana - Companies that make up the thriving and new cannabis industry comprise this grouping. They don't just cover the growth, harvest, production, and sale of the actual plant, but also things like cannabis oil products and various ingestion tools (bongs, pipes, and e-cigs). In addition, things made from byproducts of the plant like hemp fabric, fuel (can cross over into biotech), and hemp protein food products. Cannabis was first legalized in Uruguay in 2013 and Canada in 2018, with many other countries discussing it. As for the USA, the states vary (as shown in the below chart from Map of Marijuana).

State	Legal Status	Medicinal	Decriminalized
Alabama	Fully Illegal	No	No
Alaska	Fully Legal	Yes	Yes
Arizona	Mixed	Yes	No
Arkansas	Mixed	Yes	No
California	Fully Legal	Yes	Yes
Colorado	Fully Legal	Yes	Yes
Connecticut	Mixed	Yes	Reduced
Delaware	Mixed	Yes	Reduced
District of Columbia	Fully Legal	Yes	Yes

Florida	Mixed	Yes	No
Georgia	Mixed	Yes	No
Hawaii	Mixed	Yes	No
Idaho	Fully Illegal	No	No
Illinois	Mixed	Yes	Reduced
Indiana	Fully Illegal	No	No
Iowa	Fully Illegal	No	No
Kansas	Fully Illegal	No	No
Kentucky	Fully Illegal	No	No
Louisiana	Mixed	Yes	No
Maine	Fully Legal	Yes	Yes
Maryland	Mixed	Yes	Reduced
Massachusetts	Fully Legal	Yes	Yes
Michigan	Fully Legal	Yes	Yes

Minnesota	Mixed	Yes	Reduced
Mississippi	Fully Illegal	No	Reduced
Missouri	Mixed	Yes	Reduced
Montana	Mixed	Yes	No
Nebraska	Fully Illegal	No	Reduced
Nevada	Fully Legal	Yes	Yes
New Hampshire	Mixed	Yes	Reduced
New Jersey	Mixed	Yes	No
New Mexico	Mixed	Yes	Reduced
New York	Mixed	Yes	Reduced
North Carolina	Fully Illegal	No	Reduced
North Dakota	Mixed	Yes	No
Ohio	Mixed	Yes	Reduced
Oklahoma	Mixed	Yes	No

Oregon	Fully Legal	Yes	Yes
Pennsylvania	Mixed	Yes	No
Rhode Island	Mixed	Yes	Reduced
South Carolina	Fully Illegal	No	No
South Dakota	Fully Illegal	No	No
Tennessee	Fully Illegal	No	No
Texas	Fully Illegal	No	No
Utah	Mixed	Yes	No
Vermont	Fully Legal	Yes	Yes
Virginia	Fully Illegal	No	No
Washington	Fully Legal	Yes	Yes
West Virginia	Mixed	Yes	No
Wisconsin	Fully Illegal	No	No
Wyoming	Fully Illegal	No	No

As you may guess this is still rather volatile as it is not fully legal in the USA and has only just started on the international front, but the outlook is bright with news that North American sales of cannabis and related products topped 6.7 billion in 2016. Colorado and California alone generated 226 million and 345 million, respectively, in additional taxes during the tax year 2018. These numbers have been increasing by a rate of 30% every year in both sales and taxes. It is evident that both the private and public sector already see the potential to generate money with marijuana and that full legalization is on the distant horizon.

In addition, the sale of non-Tetrahydrocannabinol (THC-the enzyme that produces the high in marijuana) marijuana is readily available in all 50 states and in many countries in which the full substance is still illegal. Revenue from the sale of these products is expected to hit 22 billion by 2022. Edibles and oils made with Cannabis oil have been cited as an essential oil and are considered very beneficial in treating things like:

1. Anxiety/depression-initial tests in animals and humans show that applying the oil can calm panic attacks and help prevent them.

2. Pain-the anti-inflammatory properties of the oil have been shown to help reduce chronic pain by up to 15% in humans.

3. Heart Health-initial testing reveals that the application of a few drops has been able to reduce the inflammation that can contribute to cardiovascular events.

4. Nausea-it has been shown that the oil can help reduce feelings of uneasiness and nausea by 9%.

5. Skin Ailments-the oil is undergoing studies that show it may help reduce skin irritation and clear acne.

6. Antipsychotic Effects-studies suggest that CBD may help people by reducing psychotic symptoms.

7. Substance Abuse Treatment-CBD has been shown to modify circuits in the brain related to drug addiction and reduce substance dependence.

8. Anti-tumor Effects-in test-tube and animal studies CBD has demonstrated that it can slow the spread of breast, prostate, brain, colon and lung cancer.

9. Diabetes Prevention-in mice it reduced the incidence/symptoms of diabetes by 56%.

The uses of the related Cannabis Plant Protein called Hemp are also a source of great economic and societal boons as we are discovering more and more about it. Sales of Hemp products are estimated to be at 2.6 Billion by 2022 and cover a variety of markets and uses like:

1. Pet Food-the protein has shown great promise in the production of animal feed by using the heavy and easily digestible protein in pet food, especially for those with sensitive stomachs.

2. Human Food-the protein can make a variety of things for human consumption as it is full of amino acids. Vegan and vegetarian products like powders and faux meats are already made of hemp and things like salad dressings, cooking oils, and flour can be made from the seeds.

3. Fabric-hemp has been shown to be capable of being made into sturdy fabrics to produce clothes/bedding/industrial materials.

4. Oil Bases-hemp seed oil can be reduced to a pure oil to serve as a lubricant for industrial use and as a base for consumer products like lotions.

5. Fuel-the fuel industry has long been doing research on the use of hemp as a fossil fuel alternative. Currently, it's being used in biodiesel and ethanol.

6. Paper-paper made from hemp is of high quality and the production of hemp is much easier and take up less space than other paper/food producing plants.

7. Concrete-hemp particles can provide the base for a form of cement that is just as strong as other types. It is currently being used in home construction.

The sale of Marijuana-Related accessories and products has already topped 20 million per year in the USA alone, so it is also a booming market. The breakdown of products is shown below from Marijuana Business Daily.

Chart of the Week

Marijuana
Business Daily

Cannabis Entrepreneurs' Outlook For The Next 12 Months By Sector

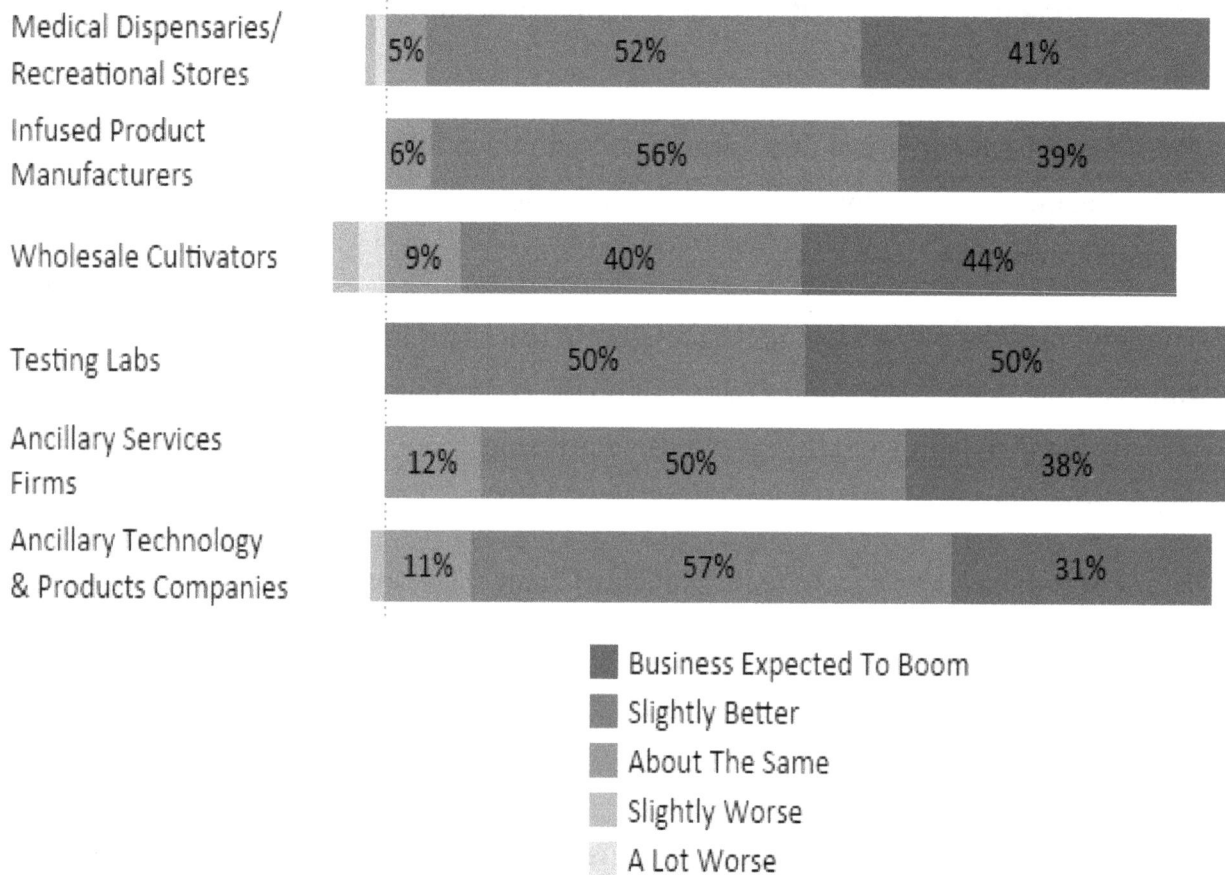

Sector			
Medical Dispensaries/ Recreational Stores	5%	52%	41%
Infused Product Manufacturers	6%	56%	39%
Wholesale Cultivators	9%	40%	44%
Testing Labs		50%	50%
Ancillary Services Firms	12%	50%	38%
Ancillary Technology & Products Companies	11%	57%	31%

- Business Expected To Boom
- Slightly Better
- About The Same
- Slightly Worse
- A Lot Worse

Source: Marijuana Business Factbook 2016

3.Cloud Technology-the process and tools that allow for transfer and storage of information. Anything that stores or allows you to pull/transmit/share information (including e-commerce) from the web is included in this category. The big boys like Apple, Microsoft, Amazon, and Google are part of this sector. The types of products in this sector include software, hardware, and online offerings, as demonstrated by the below graphic from computing.com.

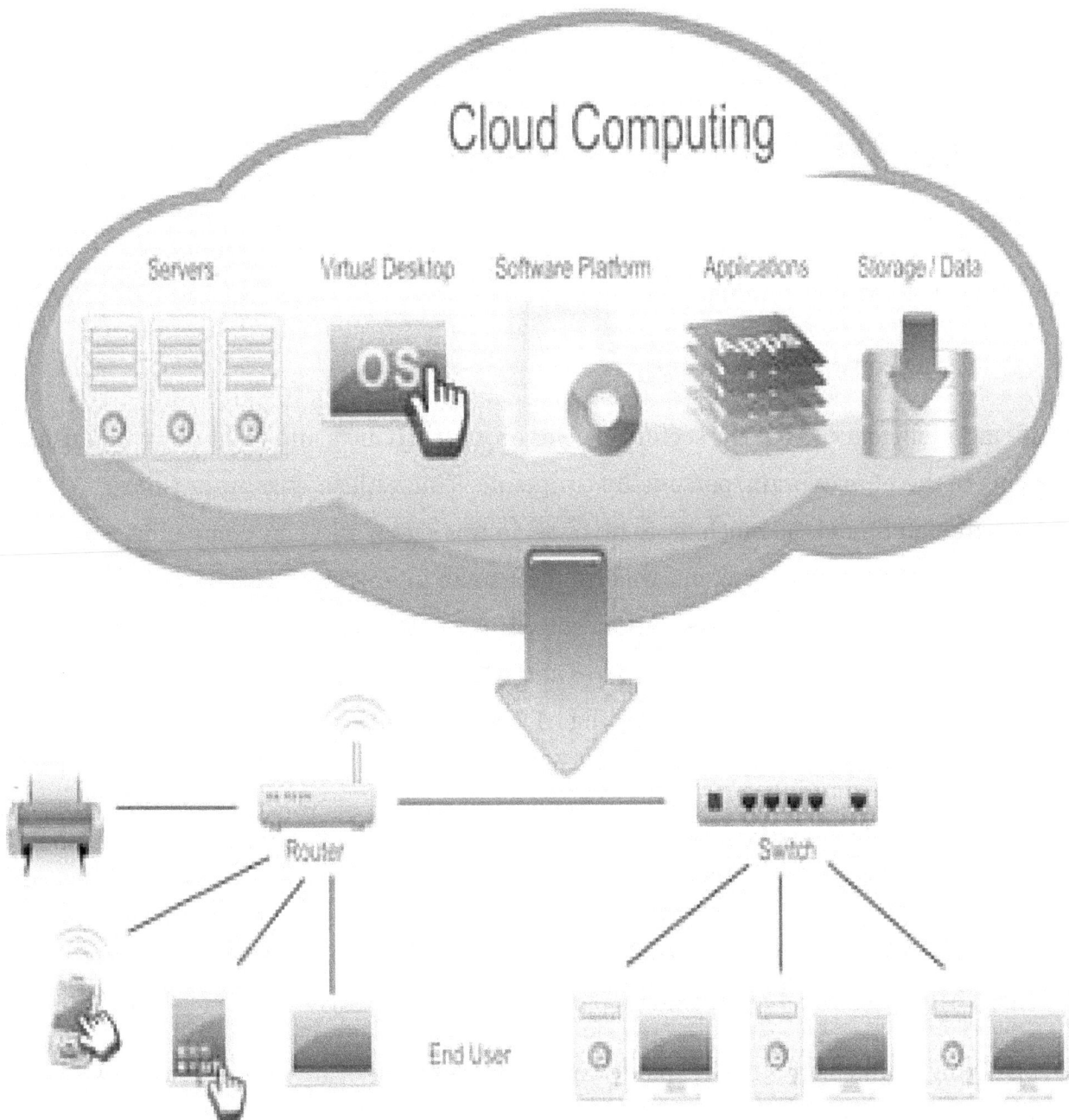

No matter what age or technological level you are at you use cloud computing, and this list will give you some idea of how far-reaching it is. The use of cloud technology is becoming the norm and is no longer an extra feature. Costly and bulky options like disc related software and storage have virtually been eliminated in favor of more efficient and less space restrictive options. Sales of cloud technology made up 85% of total IT sales in 2017 and represent a 200 billion dollar industry. Cloud computing services provide users with a series of functions including:

- Email

- Storage, backup, and data retrieval

- Creating and testing apps

- Analyzing data

- Audio and video streaming

- Delivering software on demand

4. Artificial Intelligence (AI)-This sector revolves around products and technology that use mimicking of the human brain/personality to operate. Think Alexa, Bigsby, or Google Assistant, though there is so much more involved in this sector and new companies are emerging every day with new systems that mimic human interaction. These technologies are breaking into industries like transportation, software, e-commerce, and security. Sales and development of AI topped 108 Billion in 2018 and AI is one of the fastest growing sectors in the world. Predictions state that the following AI based industries as going to grow by at least 50% in the next 50 years:

1. Accounting-taxes and basic bookkeeping will be done by software. I mean think about it, when was the last time you went to a physical tax preparer?

2. Finance/Brokerage-most if not all investing will be done online, the onset of technology has virtually eliminated the middle person or broker.

3. Banking-online banks have exploded and teller-less banks are already becoming the norm with over 80% of deposits and transactions are done using ATMs, on Apps, or online.

4. Pharmaceuticals-using AI to tabulate the data side of research will become the norm, as well as robotic solutions in compounding elements in the lab.

5. Design-AI will soon do the majority of design tabulations for certain industries by generating precise models for blueprints and sketches.

6. Government Planning-AI will become the basis for things like smart cities and we may even become able to vote online.

7. Telecommunications-automated bill payment, payment arrangements, and even changing your plan is already becoming the norm. When was the last time you paid the extra fee to speak with a person?

8. Purchasing-AI will soon make it possible to do automatic reordering of supplies or even to predict what is needed for a particular time span. This is already used in the restaurant industry with interactive Point of Sale, but it is being adapted for other industries as well.

9. Insurance/investments-purchasing of insurance online is already the standard, as well as making payments and making changes via many apps. In fact, new technologies allow rates to be set by tracking your actual driving behavior rather than age groups.

10. Medical Records-digital medical records have been the standard since 2005.

11. Health Care-new AI will allow surgeons to do more complex procedures by mapping down to the nano-cell and are even capable of doing some procedures on their own.

12. Transportation-self driving cars and trucks are being tested and will hit the roads within 50 years. Tesla and Uber are already testing autonomous vehicles in several cities.

See some examples below from AI.com.

Artificial Intelligence trends in 2019

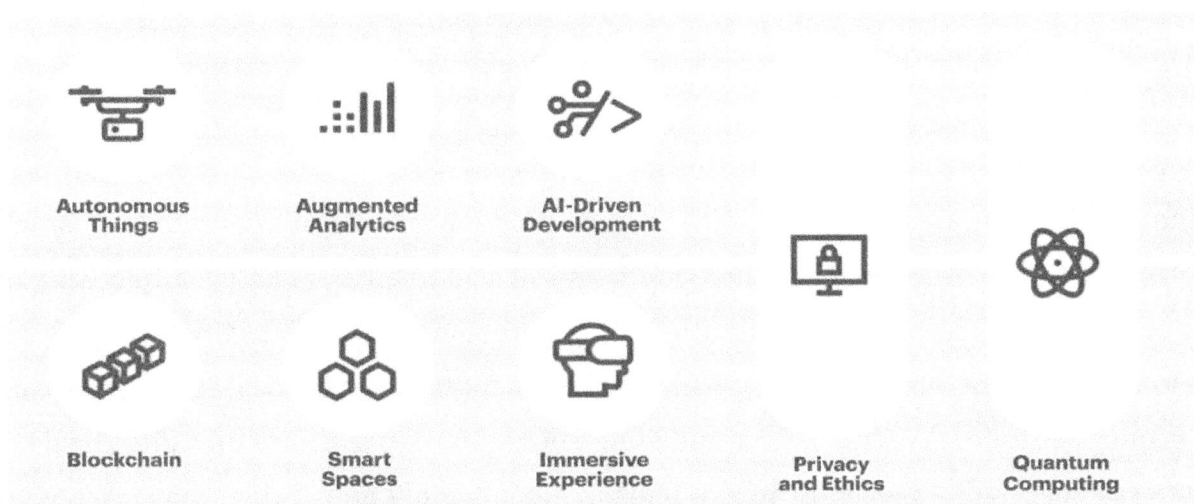

| Autonomous Things | Augmented Analytics | AI-Driven Development | | |
| Blockchain | Smart Spaces | Immersive Experience | Privacy and Ethics | Quantum Computing |

5. 5G Cellular and Wireless-5G stands for the 5th generation of wireless technology and holds promises of speeds 100 times faster than 4G and 10 times faster than the best broadband. In the next 50 years, we will see this technology lead to autonomous vehicles, smart cities, smart factories, and much more. The download, upload, and data transfer to all devices will be seamless and further merge the global economy into a more cohesive unit. Revenue from the development and sale of 5G already tops 15.7 billion and growing. Not everyone has made the jump to 5G, but all will eventually come on board with major players like Verizon, AT&T, Sprint, China Mobile, Cisco, and Google leading the pack. The estimates are 326 billion dollars in capital will be needed to establish 5g by 2025 and to be a part of most industries by 2026. These companies will continue to experience growth and investors will be rewarded.

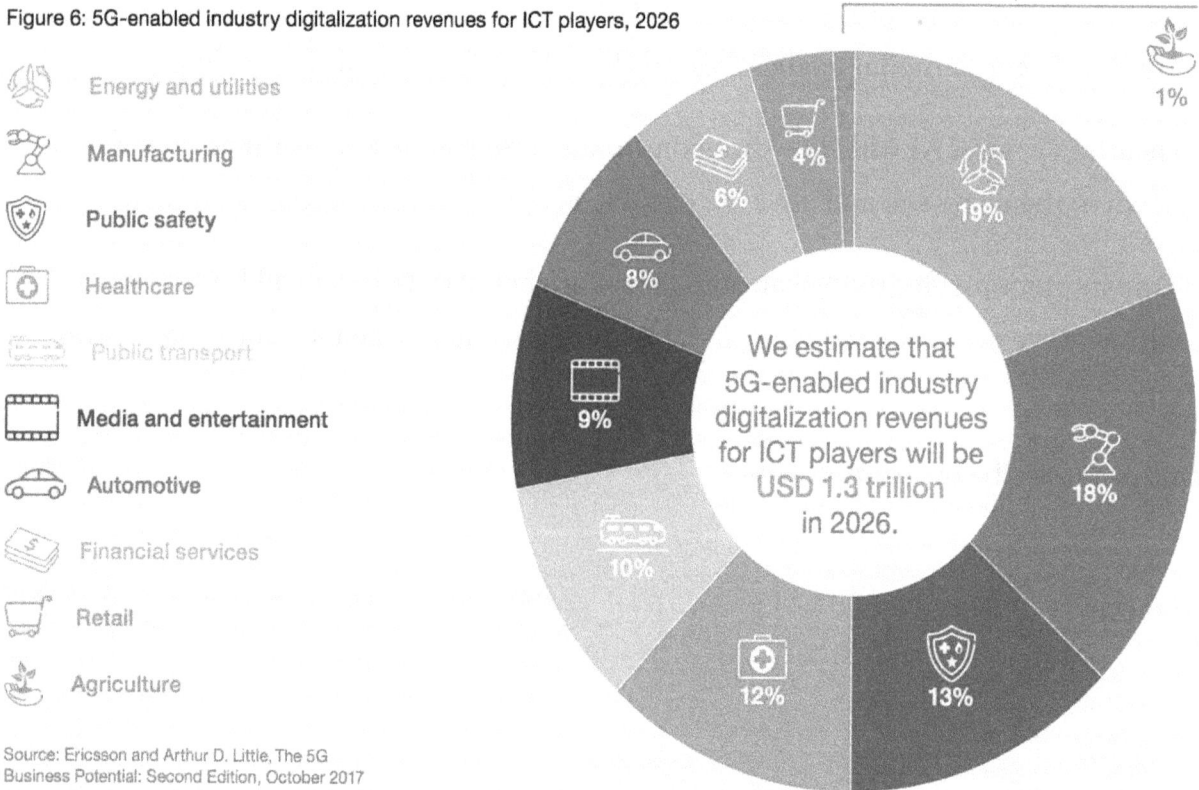

Figure 6: 5G-enabled industry digitalization revenues for ICT players, 2026

Energy and utilities

Manufacturing

Public safety

Healthcare

Public transport

Media and entertainment

Automotive

Financial services

Retail

Agriculture

We estimate that 5G-enabled industry digitalization revenues for ICT players will be USD 1.3 trillion in 2026.

Source: Ericsson and Arthur D. Little, The 5G Business Potential: Second Edition, October 2017

6. Nanotechnology-is a sector dealing with the manipulation and research of extremely small particles of 100 nanometers or less. These particles will lead to greater energy output with less strain on resources. The possibilities for the use of nano-energy in green technologies are endless and represent the hope of what will become the future technological standard as we must reduce dependence on fossil fuels and other energy sources that take up a great deal of resources or space. Also, the ability to manipulate cellular components will propel research into genetic conditions and diseases like cancer in the future, as we can possibly cure or

prevent them with the use of nanotechnology. In addition, the manipulation of microparticles of many different elements has a wide variety of consumer and personal uses as shown below.

1. **Medicine**-Nanotechnology is already being used in medicine to deliver nanoparticles that contain drugs or other substances, or that target heat or light to microorganisms and diseased cells such as cancer cells. As well as the manipulation of stem cells and other genetic material to treat and prevent disease.

2. **Electronics**-Nano electronics have already developed space saving capabilities as their weight and power consumption are significantly less than traditional electronics.

3. **Environment**-Nanotechnology has many applications aimed at improving the environment such as cleaning up polluted areas through the use of waste eating microbes or improving manufacturing methods to prevent unnecessary waste.

4. **Consumer Products**-Nanotechnology has already found its way into numerous consumer products such as skin care with micro delivery of vitamins and making fabrics flame resistant by coating fibers.

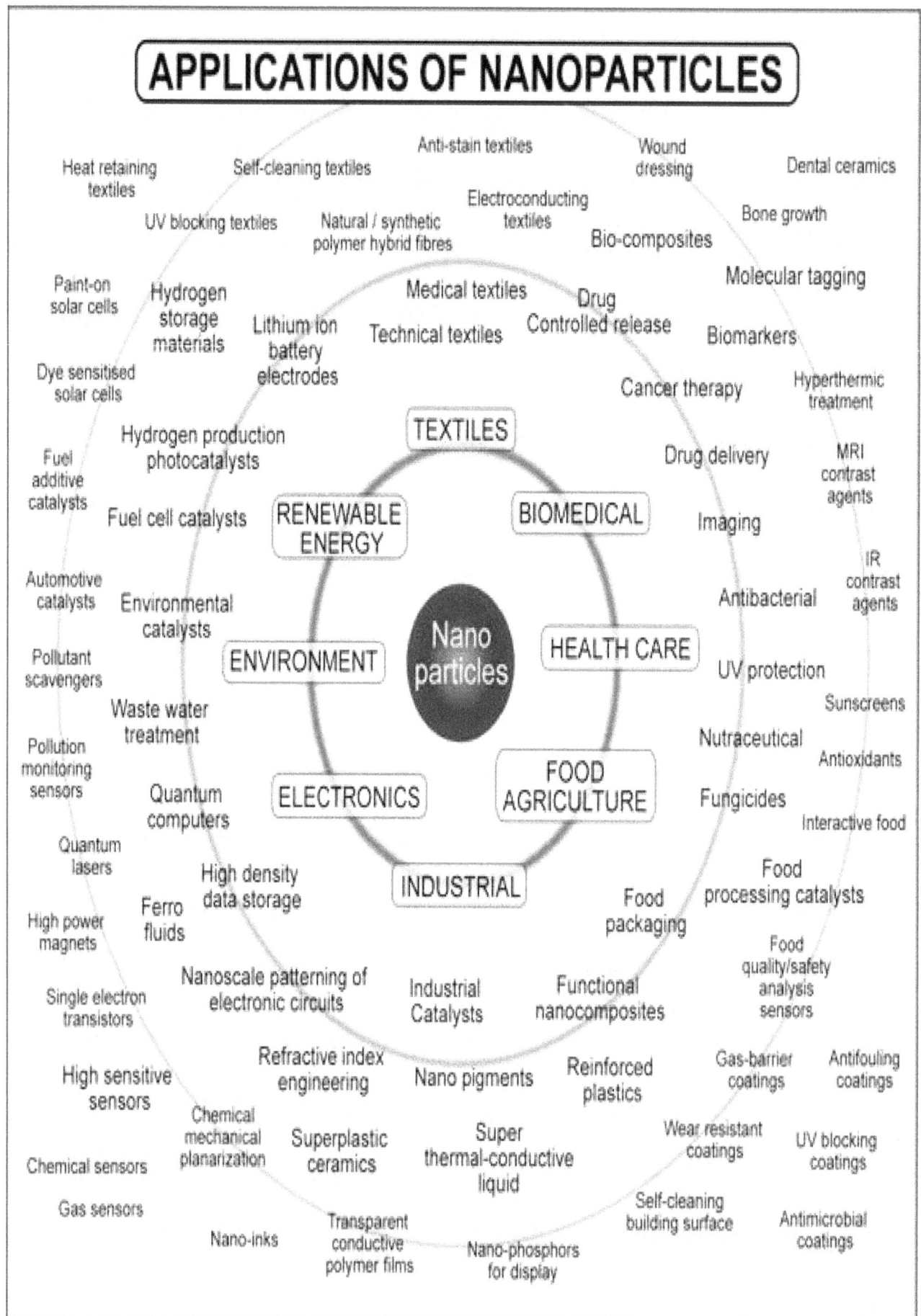

APPLICATIONS OF NANOPARTICLES

Anti-stain textiles

Wound dressing

Heat retaining textiles

Self-cleaning textiles

Dental ceramics

Electroconducting textiles

Bone growth

UV blocking textiles

Natural / synthetic polymer hybrid fibres

Bio-composites

Medical textiles

Molecular tagging

Paint-on solar cells

Hydrogen storage materials

Lithium ion battery electrodes

Technical textiles

Drug Controlled release

Biomarkers

Dye sensitised solar cells

Cancer therapy

Hyperthermic treatment

TEXTILES

Hydrogen production photocatalysts

Drug delivery

MRI contrast agents

Fuel additive catalysts

RENEWABLE ENERGY

BIOMEDICAL

Fuel cell catalysts

Imaging

IR contrast agents

Automotive catalysts

Environmental catalysts

Nano particles

Antibacterial

Pollutant scavengers

ENVIRONMENT

HEALTH CARE

UV protection

Sunscreens

Waste water treatment

Nutraceutical

Antioxidants

Pollution monitoring sensors

FOOD AGRICULTURE

Fungicides

Interactive food

Quantum computers

ELECTRONICS

Quantum lasers

Food processing catalysts

High density data storage

INDUSTRIAL

Food packaging

High power magnets

Ferro fluids

Food quality/safety analysis sensors

Single electron transistors

Nanoscale patterning of electronic circuits

Industrial Catalysts

Functional nanocomposites

High sensitive sensors

Refractive index engineering

Nano pigments

Reinforced plastics

Gas-barrier coatings

Antifouling coatings

Chemical mechanical planarization

Superplastic ceramics

Super thermal-conductive liquid

Wear resistant coatings

UV blocking coatings

Chemical sensors

Gas sensors

Nano-inks

Transparent conductive polymer films

Nano-phosphors for display

Self-cleaning building surface

Antimicrobial coatings

Chapter Two Value Stocks

How are Value Stocks Defined

Value stocks are stocks that have solid fundamentals and are priced well below their competitors in their respective fields. The determination of the "value of the stock" is based on the opinions of Wall Street Analysts, Brokers, and Peers in the same industry. As you can probably guess, this is highly speculative and not an exact science. The primary thing to remember is that value stocks are not always growth stocks. The stock is measured on its intrinsic value or true value based on factors such as its profits, P & L, stability, and potential for future growth. These are determined by many different methods and will vary by a few dollars analyst to analyst. Most of these companies will offer dividends or shares of their profits in good quarters to investors which is another source of profit and an enticement to choose the company's stock. This type of trading (with the exception of dividends) is true for not only stocks but bonds and commodities such as sugar and coffee on their own markets. These are stocks that provide income in ways other than just capital gains from sale or stock price. Though that appreciation is present, holders of value stock are more concerned with getting cash for dividends and bonuses.

Here are a few questions to ask a broker about value stocks:

- What is the status of your fund and how is it structured, do you specialize in value vs growth stocks?

- Do you have a specific industry or geographic focus for your investments and how much value is expected for value stocks?

- What are your most successful investments and what is their payout history?

- What metrics are you tracking when considering an investment in a value stock and do you keep accurate records of the payouts?

- How many investments do you make per year, and what is your typical investment size?

If you are interested, here is a list of the top value stocks of the current year

1. Eaton (ETN, $69.11) which is priced at less than 15 times trailing profits and roughly 12 times next year's projected earnings.

Stephen Satoshi

2. FedEx (FDX, $173.96) is still a solid business, but its growth is limited in the delivery industry.

3. Allstate (ALL, $86.49) lost almost a quarter of its value between late September and Christmas, prompted in large part by Hurricane Florence battering the East Coast and Hurricane Michael hitting the Gulf Coast.

4. AT&T (T, $30.67) is down roughly 30% from its 2016 peak, reaching fresh multi-year lows in December before bouncing back to still-depressed levels.

5. Pentair (PNR, $40.54) shares broadly continued the downward trek they began shortly before the recent spinoff was even announced.

6. Electronic Arts (EA, $90.47) is down nearly 40% of their value since their peak in 2018.

7. Caterpillar (CAT, $124.37) – Many experts say that the new tariffs and other trade regulations will cause this market price to drop, but that the dividends and other perks will make this a key value stock

8. Bank of America (BAC, $29.63) has dipped below $23 twice in the last year, but the fact that its day to day operations remain strong makes this great for income, but not growth.

9. AbbVie (ABBV, $77.14) has had a rough 2018 but overall have had some peaks and valleys that raised the price to back above $38 per share.

Value Trading vs Growth Trading

The strategy of value investing/trading was created in the 1930s by David Dodd and Ben Graham (Ivy League Finance Professors) with the publishing of their book, "Security Analysis" which has become the standard for all analysis. Until the 21st century, most traditional investing was based on value investing and relied on "reading charts" to guess what the future value of a stock would be. The intrinsic value (guessed value) minus the market price is the margin of safety and most investors would practice the risky technique of betting the stock will stay in the safety zone to make money. If you buy at the value price and then it climbs to the intrinsic price on the market then you win, if it falls below the purchase price you lose.

To protect themselves some value investors use an even more complicated hedge system of "puts" and "calls" to protect themselves in value investing. This is done on a secondary market that bundles the calls or puts them into another type of security. It consists of buying a call option on the stock or the right to buy at a low price (to protect themselves from buying high) or a put option that permits them to sell at a certain price (to protect from selling low). So, to have this type of insurance one must buy the stock, then purchase a call or put on a secondary market to "hedge" their bet on the stock. If the designated price or strike price is reached then the investor can use the hedge and someone will sell to them or buy from them at the strike price. The investor who owns the stock has the right to any gains on the stock price and any dividends, while those on the secondary market of puts and calls do not.

Wow, that all sounds complicated and it is. That is why I highly recommended the simpler method of buying growth stocks and making your profits from the rise in the price. The use of Hedge and Value Investing gave rise to the behemoth of Wall Street that you see in movies about the 1980s. This was where investment banks and brokers made their money and in many ways caused the recession of 2007. They took the model of the secondary "put and call" options and expanded it to selling things like mortgages as securities. This created a huge "middle person" giant of those that took the orders from clients and executed the trades or secondary trades.

Options may seem overwhelming, but they're actually very easy to understand if you know how to look at them. As you learn more, you may realize this is not the type of investing you are interested in, but I feel a thorough understanding of both types is needed to grow as an investor. Yes, you are starting as a simple growth investor, but as your money and expertise grow so will your interest in other types of investments. Most complex or mixed portfolios are usually constructed with several asset classes. These may be stocks, bonds, ETFs, mutual funds, preferred stocks, and alternative investments. Options are just another asset class, and when used properly, they offer many advantages to other types of investing.

They are powerful because they enhance a portfolio with added income, protection, and leverage. There is usually an option that is appropriate for any investor's goal. Often (as previously mentioned) they are used as a guard or hedge against a declining stock market or instrument to limit losses. They can also be used to produce monthly or quarterly income.

As with other types of investments, there is no guarantee with options. Trading them involves certain risks that the investor must be aware of before making a trade. In fact, you often see them sold with this or other types of disclaimers.

"Options involve risks and are not suitable for everyone. Options trading can be speculative in nature and carry substantial risk of loss." (Source Investopedia)

Most options belong to securities known as derivatives, which are often associated with risk-taking and massive speculations. Think the speculation on home mortgages prior to 2008, they were a form of derivative. However, the overall bad perception of derivatives is really overblown. Derivative means that its price is dependent on the price of something else. Options are derivatives of other types of stocks and investments and are therefore dependent on them. On the overall standard, a stock option typically represents 100 shares of the stock.

If you buy or sell an option contract it grants you the right to buy or sell the contract but does not require you to move on the underlying asset at a set price on or before a certain date. Call options give the holder the right to buy a stock (as bundles in an option) and a put gives the holder the right to sell a stock (as bundled in the option).

To demonstrate the two types of options look at the following:

For a call option, an investor gets wind of a potential extra offering of a marijuana stock. The investor decided he or she wants the right to purchase that stock in the future, depending on certain parameters that are advantageous to the investor. These circumstances would affect their decision to buy the stock, think the USA legalizing marijuana at a future date. The investor would benefit from the option of buying or not. They can buy a call option on the stock which gives them the ability to buy the stock at $10.00 per share at any point in the next three years. They secure the purchase with a nonrefundable deposit to secure the option to call (think call for the sale).

The cost or payment is the premium for the option. It is the price of the option contract. The deposit might be $30,000 that the buyer pays for the stock. Let's say three years have passed, and the USA has legalized weed and its sub-products. The investor exercises the option and buys the stock for $10 per share, even though the price has rocketed to #20 per share. However, if legalization does not happen, the investor must still buy the stock at 10 per share, even if the price is hovering around 8 to 11 per share. That is the contract. The 30k premium is still kept as that was the price for the right to buy.

Now, as to a put option, if you own the Marijuana Stock a put option would be an insurance policy on the value of the stock in the future. The investor may fear that a bear (down) market is near and may be unwilling to lose more than 10% of their position in the stock. If the stock is currently trading at $10 per share, they can buy a put option giving the right to sell the index at 9.90 per share, at any point in the designated time period.

If the price falls to 7 in the next few years they limited their losses to 10% or pennies on the share and if the stock goes up, they are under no obligation to sell at 9.90 per share. Therefore they only lose the premium paid, unless they can later sell at a higher price.

Buying a stock instantly gives you a long position while buying a call option gives you a possible long position in the stock. If you sell a naked or uncovered call, this gives you a possible short position in the underlying stock. However, buying a put option gives you a possible short position on the stock. Selling a naked position in a put gives you a possible long position in the stock. Keeping these four possibilities straight in your head is crucial.

Finally, to understand options here are some general terms you must know.

The seller of an option is called its writer

The strike price of an option contract is the agreed price the stock in question is bought or sold.

When an option is in-the-money it means the buyer came out on the positive end of the contract.

The expiration date is the precise date that the option contract terminates.

Options can be traded on a national options exchange, such as the Chicago Board Options Exchange or CBOE, those are called listed options.

These types of options have fixed strike prices and expiration dates and each contract represents 100 shares of a stock.

The amount which an option is in-the-money is its intrinsic value.

When an option is out-of-the-money the option for the buyer is on the negative end of the purchase or sell.

The total cost or price of an option is the premium and is dependent on:

1. Stock price

2. Strike price

3. Time remaining until expiration (time value)

4. Volatility or history of the movement of the stock

Speculation is a wager or bet on the future price direction of a stock and of the derivative that the option is based on.

Hedging with options is meant to reduce risk at a reasonable cost, think of an insurance policy for stocks, this is an option.

Spreads are the difference between the strike price and purchase price.

Combinations are trades constructed with both a call and a put.

An option is the potential to participate in a future price change. So, if you own a call, you can participate in the upward movement of a stock without owning the stock. You have the option to participate or not to participate, based on your best interests.

For many of us, a middle-man is necessary in a value-based system because of the expertise required to make money. This type of expertise is something most of us do not have and we fare better in a simpler system. The secondary market has largely gone away on Wall Street with the advent of new technologies that allow the common person to trade from a computer or smartphone directly with the market, without a middle person.

Though some middle experts are needed for larger transactions, for most of us the simplicity of trading today is adequate. This new simple method is known as the Growth Market and is what we will concentrate on. Also within the realm of Value Trading is the market (Pink Sheets) that involve very small companies known as "Penny Stocks", they are companies with very cheap prices that the investor feels are poised to grow exponentially.

Bigger companies can have inflated prices since everyone's paying attention to them, while small-cap stocks tend to have fewer people that even know about them. Less risky investors stay away from them since they tend to be risky and most group investors (mutual funds) have restrictions when it comes to investing in them. They are more volatile and therefore difficult to trade.

Basics of Growth Investing

Remember you only need to be right once or twice (1000%+ returns) to secure financial freedom for the rest of your life and we will be looking at the stocks and stock strategy that can make that happen. In contrast to value investors, growth investors buy stock in companies that may be trading for more than their intrinsic or estimated value. They make decisions based on the same charts, but with the added element of market trends and past market performance. The growth investor assumes that the price or value (no matter what it is) will grow over the long term and bring them profit with the spread between the purchase price and future value. This is why people buy 500 shares of Apple or Google at 200 plus dollars a share because they see the potential for a modest profit in the future. If you choose correctly over a volume of trades that modest profit turns into a huge profit. Ultimately, growth investors seek to increase their profit through capital appreciation, much like those that flip houses or cars. The profit is in the resale price.

Growth investors seek to invest in companies whose earnings are expected to grow at a faster rate than the rest of the market average or the average of their own sectors. So they tend to focus on younger/newer companies or proven companies with growth potential. Their theory is that positive performance by the company in their actual operations will equate to better market performance and higher returns on the price of their stock. Most of these companies (as we pointed out in chapter one) are in the growth or hot industries that are developing the technologies, services, and products that will become popular or essentials in the future. The focus is entirely on growth in the stock price not on the payout of investor dividends since most of these growing companies reinvest their earnings rather than paying investors or executives.

Predicting the hot growth companies is not an exact science and it requires some case by case interpretation and judgment. No matter what method you utilize it takes a degree of both gambling instinct and hard past performance data. Investors use certain criteria as a framework for their analysis, but these methods must be applied with the company's individual situation in mind. No two companies are alike even if they operate in the same sector or develop competing products. For example, Apple and Samsung both dominate smartphone sales but are very different companies and offer products for very different types of consumers. They must each be considered on their own, apart from each other or other producers of smartphones or wireless products.

Growth stocks trade on any exchange and in any sector, but you'll usually find them in the current growth industries (which we highlighted in chapter one). However, there are some average guidelines you might use to point out yet unrecognized growth companies to invest in.

- Strong historical earnings growth. Companies should show a track record of strong earnings growth over the previous five to 10 years. The minimum EPS growth depends on the size of the company, but returns or growth that averages 3% to 10% is a good gauge. Why this range? 3% to 5% is average growth for most businesses, so choosing ones with at least that much is a good indicator of success and of course over that is just gravy. The basic idea is that if the company has displayed average to good growth in the last 5 to 10 years, it's likely to continue doing so over the next 5 to 10 years.

- Strong Earnings Reports from the company itself is a huge indicator. An earnings report is a release that outlines the company's profitability for a specific period usually for the most recently elapsed quarter or year. It's these estimates that garner a lot of attention from investors, as they are usually a great indicator of how the company will do measured against the others in the sector.

- Strong profit margins. A company's profits are calculated by deducting all expenses from sales (except taxes) and dividing by sales. It's an important metric to consider because a company can have fantastic growth in sales with poor gains in earnings. Basically, a company can show 1 billion in gross revenues, but once everything is deducted (save taxes) they may only show 10 million in earnings (taxable). This could indicate that management is not controlling costs and is allowing revenue to be eaten up by expenses. No company will survive if this ratio is off and so a company that exceeds its previous average of pretax profit margins and those of its sector could be a good growth candidate.

- Strong return on equity (ROE). This measures how much profit a company produces when compared with the money shareholders invest. It's calculated by dividing net income (revenues after taxes and expenses have been deducted) by shareholder equity (dollar amount held in shares by investors). Compare a company's present ROE to the five-year average ROE of the company and the industry. If the number is stable or increasing, then the ROE indicates that management is doing a good job protecting investor money and giving them a return on their investment (ROI).

- Strong stock performance. This is the simplest method because, in general, if a stock cannot realistically double its returns over a 10 year period than it is not a growth stock. To double in 10 years, a company's growth must be at least 7% to 10% per year for every year in the period. Some industries returns might average at a 50% growth, which only requires a 5% return year over year, so take it case by case.

Chapter Three Growth Portfolio Allocations

When investing, particularly for long-term goals, there are two things you will likely hear about frequently, Allocation and Diversification. Diversification helps buffer or limit an investors risk or exposure to loss in any one type of investment or one type of industry. Allocation or the range or mix of your investments will provide the guide or outline for your choices of investments. Truly understanding how the two work can help you comprise or build a portfolio that really meets your needs and goals, while only incurring your desired level of risk.

Generally, diversification deals with the process of investing in a number of different instruments to help negate risk. The basic idea is that if some of your investments in your portfolio lose or decline in value that others may increase or hold fast. For example, say you wanted to invest in mostly single or basic stocks, there is a way to diversify even in a single asset class (a type of investment). Rather than investing in just the stocks of American companies or companies based wherever you are in the world, you could mix up your portfolio or asset mix by investing in the stocks of companies in foreign nations, as well. Also, instead of just relying on "Blue Chip", large caps, or the stocks of well-known or older companies (think IBM, Google/Alphabet, Kraft Foods), you could mix it up by investing in startups or smaller/less well-known companies (small caps or medium caps).

For those of you that prefer the more stable instruments like bonds for income, you could choose a mix or both government and corporate bonds to potentially take advantage the higher returns on corporate bonds, while negating the risk with the more stable government issue bonds. Also, instead of relying on one type of maturity within bonds, you could mix it up on the maturity dates, with a mix of 5, 10, 20-year bonds, or even longer. Remember that longer-term bonds tend to react more dramatically to interest rate functions than shorter-term bonds. So, interest rates will have less effect on a five-year bond than a 20-year bond.

For those that wish to venture outside things like stocks and bonds, there is the world of currency trading on the FOREX. This is basically buying blocks of a foreign currency and then selling when its value increases. This requires a little more day trading and daily watching of the news and political events to grasp, but it is a great way to generate short term (less than 5 year) gains.

Asset allocation is a strategic way to align your portfolio with different asset classes that will maximize your returns while severely limiting your risk in a downturn. After researching all your investment goals, timeline, and fear or tolerance to risk. Then you would then invest different amounts of money (for a different percentage) of your portfolio in a range of different instruments to reach your goals while keeping your risk of loss down at a level you are willing to accept. A careful study and grasp of these three factors will guide your choices and help you make the right decisions.

Overall, a large profit margin or accumulation level, a high-risk tolerance, and a long timeline will usually translate into a more aggressive portfolio or a strategy with a higher concentration in more risky instrument types. This will naturally lead to more money or a higher percentage of your portfolio invested in long term growth investments. A common example of an aggressive or growth strategy is 70% stocks, 20% bonds, and 10% cash. On the flip side, a person whose goal is a shorter timeline, with less risk in exchange for more moderate gains would require a more conservative approach. Such a conservative or income-oriented strategy would be 50% bonds, 30% stocks and real estate, and 20% cash.

Just remember that over time, a portfolio's allocations can shift due to changing market performance. In bull (up) market years when the stock market performs particularly well, a portfolio may become heavy in stocks, while in years when bonds outperform, they may end up comprising a larger percentage of a portfolio. So, for the investor who wished to follow a formula, a little bit of rebalancing may be in order to compensate for the change in the market.

There are generally two ways to rebalance a portfolio. The first is by simply selling any over-weighted asset classes (instruments) and directing the proceeds into the under-weighted assets. The second is to direct new investments (assets) into the under-weighted asset class until the desired formula or balance is reached. Just remember to keep in mind that selling investments can result in taxes unless they are held in a tax-free or advantaged account. Think 401k sponsored retirement plan or an IRA. So, just make sure the gains from sales outweigh the taxes or a profit can quickly become a loss or a break even.

The following list shows how many times during the past 30 years each type of investment has fared positively in terms of performance. It helps show why diversification among asset classes is important.

Asset class	Number of winning years, 1987-2016
Cash	3
Bonds	5
Stocks	10
Foreign stocks	12

Source: Thomson Reuters, 2017.

Simply stated a good portfolio (your collection of investments) allocation will balance your return with your risk. Risk, what is risk? I didn't sign up for that. Unfortunately, you did, as nothing in the stock market is risk-free. Not only can you fail to profit but you can also lose the money you initially invested if you make the wrong choices. But hey that is why we are only starting with $100 for this book. You will learn the best way to allocate your investments to make sure you are profiting year after year. In the following chapter, we explore basic strategies that fit most investors.

Proper Allocation

Basic Types of Allocations

<u>The Profit-Driven Portfolio</u>

This portfolio focuses on making money through alternative methods like dividends or distributions to stakeholders, in addition to capital gains from the stock price. These Blue-chip or more settled companies are usually not growth stocks, but I feel compelled to mention them as you may want to add some of them as your knowledge and investment skills grow. One bright side to value stocks it that you can continue to receive dividends from them in a downturn if the company's performance is stable. The income portfolio should generate positive cash flow, bottom line. This is real cash and profits in your pocket each year. Real Estate and Bonds are usually good options for this type of portfolio, in addition to companies that return a great majority of their profits back to shareholders instead of investing all of it in growing the business. They may invest some of it into the business, but the vast majority is written off by giving it to investors for tax benefits. In this way, they pass their income through to the shareholders and pay much fewer taxes. An example of this type of company is Real Estate Investment Trusts (REITs) which pool money to flip real estate, without one person taking all the risk. Most REITs are traded on major stock exchanges, but there are also public non-listed and private REITs. The two main types of REITs are equity REITs and mortgage REITs commonly known as mREITs, but there are four major types as shown below from Reit Invester.com

Equity REITs – a company that owns or operates income-producing real estate.

Mortgage REITs – mREITs provide financing for income-producing real estate by purchasing or originating mortgages and mortgage-backed securities and earning income from the interest on these investments.

Public Non-listed REITs – PNLRs are registered with the SEC but do not trade on any major stock exchanges.

Private REITs – Private REITs are offerings that are exempt from SEC registration and whose shares do not trade on national stock exchanges.

These stocks are very tied to the economic climate, even more than most stocks, but while the real estate market is hot or rising the profits from the resales are then given back to the investors as dividends. They can take a beating when the market falls, as real estate building and buying activity dries up. So, make sure you keep abreast of this as with any non-growth stock.

This Portfolio is a nice complement to most people's salary, wage, or retirement savings. Contrary to growth investors those in this type of portfolio should look out for stocks that may have fallen out of favor but still maintain a high rate of distributions to investors. These companies not only supplement income but also provide those capital gains, as no company pays dividends if its bottom line is not healthy. In addition to REITs, bonds, utilities, and other slow-growth industries are an ideal choice for this type of portfolio.

The Aggressive Portfolio

This portfolio is as close to Reno, Vegas, or Atlantic City as you can legally get. It presents more risk than any others we will discuss. Most experts say that a maximum of 10% of one's money be used to fund this type of portfolio. Aggressive stocks can be Initial Public Offerings (IPOs) of new companies, technology or health care businesses in the process of researching a breakthrough product, or a small energy company about to release its earnings report. Aggressive Portfolios and stocks, require the most work to be traded successfully, as you do not want to buy and hold but instead to use a day trading type of strategy.

An aggressive investment strategy is generally a strategy that is designed to maximize returns by taking a relatively higher degree of risk. Strategies for achieving higher returns typically emphasize growth over time as a primary investment goal, rather than steady income or safety of your principal. This strategy would, therefore, have an investment allocation with a substantial or majority percentage in stocks or real estate and little or no investments allocated to bonds or cash.

Aggressive investment strategies are generally more suitable for young adults with smaller portfolio sizes because they usually have a lengthy investment timeline that enables them to ride out short-term market changes. They are not deterred by sudden losses early on that may have less impact than changes near the end of the timeline. Most investment advisors do not consider this strategy right for anyone else unless such a strategy is applied to only a small portion of one's total savings. Regardless of the investor's age high tolerance to risk is a prerequisite for this type of strategy. These are the key concepts of an aggressive type allocation.

- Accepts more risk in pursuit of greater return.

- Achieves its goals through one or more of many strategies including asset selection and asset allocation.

Since the 2008 recession, data shows a preference away from aggressive strategies and active management and towards passive index investing. However, for those investing aggressively, their allocation would contain the following:

Portfolio One - 75% equities and real estate, 15% fixed income, and 10% commodities.

Portfolio Two - 85% equities and real estate and 15% commodities.

Aggressive investment strategies would also utilize a higher turnover strategy, seeking to concentrate on stocks that show high return in a short time period.

Generally, an aggressive strategy needs more constant management than a conservative long-term wait and hold strategy. It is likely to be much more volatile and could require a lot of adjustments, depending on market conditions. Also, more active rebalancing would also be required to bring portfolio allocations **back to their target levels. The** volatility of the assets could lead mixes to deviate significantly from their original weights.

The Mixed Portfolio

A mixed portfolio means venturing into other types of investments outside of stocks. Bonds, commodities, real estate, and even art. There is a lot of flexibility in this approach and a lot of people prefer it. Traditionally, this type of portfolio would contain growth and income stocks, government or corporate bonds, and REITs. A common strategy for a hybrid portfolio would include a mix of stocks and bonds in relatively fixed proportions. This type of approach offers diversification across multiple types of investments and is more suited for a conservative type of investor.

The best way to accomplish a mixed allocation would be to look at the timeline we have for when we might need the money we're investing. Any investors that might need their money within a year's time should simply invest in an interest-bearing cash account. Period. Taking a chance and investing your cash (when you need it so soon) in bonds or stocks is not advantageous as there is a huge chance that a percentage of your money could be lost before you need it. Keeping the principal safe and liquid is the smart thing to do for any money that might be needed quickly.

Money should be invested only if it's going toward long-term goals further than five years out, such as retirement. The best investment for long-term growth is stocks because, over long periods of time, they outperform nearly all other types of investments. This is even though they may lose value in a given year.

Many financial advisors adhere to the rule of subtracting your age from 110. The answer should be the percentage of your portfolio that's invested in stocks. As a person ages, their portfolio's mix of stocks and bonds will gradually move to a more conservative mix. Investors can always tweak the formula to their own tastes if they are willing to accept more risk. A more aggressive investor may up the number to 120, allowing a 50-year-old to invest 70% of their portfolio in stocks. Many investors and advisors believe that if they increase their portfolio's range of allocation and diversify its stock and other instruments, they decrease its risk. This is not necessarily true, especially for those who spend time studying individual investments. It can be safe to allocate your funds into a diverse range within the sale asset class. For example a mix of common and preferred stock or a range of different industries.

Now that you have an understanding of what a portfolio is and how to allocate it, let's take a look at the various strategies they most investors use.

Recession Proof Stocks

Yes, they exist and we are going to take a quick look at what makes a recession-proof stock and how to recognize them. First recession is defined as an extended period of time where the elements of economic growth are sub-par such as:

1. GDP (Gross Domestic Product)-In the 2006/8 recession the GDP defined as: private consumption + gross investment + government investment + government spending + (exports – imports), dipped with losses of 2.5% and finally started creeping up in 2009.

2. Unemployment Rate (number of unemployed persons / labor force)-The unemployment rate grew to 4.9% during the 2006 to 2008 recession and has steadily decreased to a low of 3.4% currently.

3. Job Creation (number of new job creation in comparison to the previous period)-In the 2006 to 2008 recession we lost almost 3 million jobs compared to the current rate of over 300k added per quarter.

4. Income Levels (rates of wages to inflation)-The rate of wages to inflation has remained at a steady 7.25 per hour for minimum wage in most states. The rate is low and is the subject of much debate.

5. Inflation Rate (value of the dollar to the cost of goods)-We have remained at the core rate of 1.9% for many years with rates expected to climb to 2% in 2021 to 2022.

6. Strength of the Dollar (value of the dollar to other currencies)-The dollar has had a bit of roller coaster over the past 10 years, but still remains a powerful element in the world

market.

With those ideas in mind, it is common sense that recession-proof stocks would be those that either assist "Main Street" with saving money or escaping the worry or stress that inevitably accompany a recession. Also, necessities like Food, Utilities, and basic transportation needs are pretty much recession proof. Here are the top recession-proof stocks that remained at least 2% (beating core inflation) growth during downturns:

- COSTCO (COST)-Current Stock Price-$243 per share, Lowest Price During Recession $189 per share

- Sam's Club and Walmart (WMT)-Current Stock Price-$102 per share, Lowest Price During Recession-$95 per share

- Walt Disney (DIS)-Current Stock Price-$133 per share, Lowest Price During Recession-$115 per share

- Netflix (NFLX)-Current Stock Price-$375 per share, Lowest Price During Recession-$325 per share

- Dollar General (DG)-Current Stock Price-$122 per share, Lowest Price During Recession-$115 per share

- Big Lots (BIG)-Current Stock Price-$37 per share, Lowest Price During Recession-$28 per share

- Spirit Airlines (SAVE)-Current Stock Price-$55 per share, Lowest Price During Recession-$50 per Share

- Molson Coors (TAP)-Current Stock Price-$60 per share, Lowest Price During Recession-$52 per share

- Constellation (marijuana) (STZ)-Current Stock Price-$205, Lowest Price During Recession (N/A)

- Canopy Growth (CGC)-Current Stock Price-$47 per share, Lowest Price During Recession (N/A)

- Cell Phone Carriers: T-Mobile (TMUS) Verizon (VZ) AT&T (T) Sprint (S) Current Stock

Prices-73, 56, 31, & 5 per share, all of them held to at least 2% growth during 2006 to 2008

- Public Storage PSA S&P 500 lost 55% from 2007 - 2009; PSA shares lost 38%

- Brookfield Infrastructure Partners (BIP) S&P 500 lost 51% in 2008; BIP shares lost 43% (IPO'd in 2008)

Other stocks remained strong investments during the recession through the growth of their dividends:

- Duke Energy (DUK) S&P 500 lost 55% from 2007 - 2009; DUK shares lost 34%

  o Dividend Growth Streak: 11 years

- Digital Realty Trust (DLR) S&P 500 lost 55% from 2007 - 2009; DLR shares lost 27%

  o Dividend Growth Streak: 13 years

- WEC Energy Group (WEC) S&P 500 lost 55% from 2007 - 2009; WEC shares lost 18%

  o Dividend Growth Streak: 15 years

- Flowers Foods (FLO) S&P 500 lost 55% from 2007 - 2009; FLO shares lost 1%

  o Dividend Growth Streak: 16 years

- Magellan Midstream Partners (MMP) S&P 500 lost 55% from 2007 - 2009; MMP shares lost 30%

  o Dividend Growth Streak: 17 years

- Enterprise Products Partners (EPD) S&P 500 lost 55% from 2007 - 2009; EPD shares lost 37%

  o Dividend Growth Streak: 20 years

- Reality Income Corp (O) S&P 500 lost 55% from 2007 - 2009; O shares lost 43%

  o Dividend Growth Streak: 24 years

- Chevron (CVX) S&P 500 lost 55% from 2007 - 2009; CVX shares lost 34%

- o Dividend Growth Streak: 32 years

- Exxon Mobil Corporation (XOM) S&P 500 lost 55% from 2007 - 2009; XOM shares lost 28%

  - o Dividend Growth Streak: 35 years

- Consolidated Edison (ED) S&P 500 lost 55% from 2007 - 2009; ED shares lost 26%

  - o Dividend Growth Streak: 44 years

- Pepsico (PEP) S&P 500 lost 55% from 2007 - 2009; PEP shares lost 35%

  - o Dividend Growth Streak: 45 years

- Kimberly-Clark (KMB) S&P 500 lost 55% from 2007 - 2009; KMB shares lost 34%

  - o Dividend Growth Streak: 45 years

- Leggett & Platt (LEG) S&P 500 lost 55% from 2007 - 2009; LEG shares lost 44%

  - o Dividend Growth Streak: 46 years

- Altria (MO) S&P 500 lost 55% from 2007 - 2009; MO shares lost 20%

  - o Dividend Growth Streak: 49 years

- Coca-Cola (KO) S&P 500 lost 55% from 2007 - 2009; KO shares lost 31%

  - o Dividend Growth Streak: 55 years

- Johnson & Johnson (JNJ) S&P 500 lost 55% from 2007 - 2009; JNJ shares lost 27%

  - o Dividend Growth Streak: 56 years

- Procter & Gamble (PG) S&P 500 lost 55% from 2007 - 2009; PG shares lost 36%

  - o Dividend Growth Streak: 61 years

Do you see the pattern of necessity and escape in these stocks? Keep that in mind during the next downturn with the noted characteristics of these types of stocks:

1. *The company provides critical repair/maintenance/essentials*-Consumers cut out

optional services first and identify things they can do themselves instead of hiring them out. Think about household repairs, landscaping, or house cleaning.

2. *The company serves an elite or protected client*-These are both the very rich who will continue their luxuries and those somewhat protected from the recession. Think food delivery to grocers, supplies to utility plants, and medical and pharmaceutical suppliers.

3. *The company provides products or services that are the rule of law*-They provide their services or products to people or business that run under a government mandate. Think police, fire, EMS and those that supply them, and the military.

4. *The Company provides escape or needed stress relief*-This seems trivial, but alcohol, marijuana, and home-based entertainment companies usually remain stable during times of recession. See the above list of recession-proof stocks for examples.

5. *The company provides discounted essentials or is built on bargains*-Think stores and businesses that are known for providing cheap or heavily discounted products. The list of stocks above represents discount retailers and travel providers.

The Basic Investment Strategies

1. Value Investing

This is the investment strategy we looked at in chapter two which is based on finding stocks that are underpriced or undervalued. The amount of chart reading and research this takes is staggering and the returns can be very slow. This a buy and hold that requires a long-term investor who is content with holding onto a stock for years to get a payoff.

2. Income or Profit Investing

This strategy involves going heavy into Profit Stocks/Portfolios that involve companies that pay distributions and capital gains on resale price. They can provide a reliable income stream with minimal risk and because they are a long term hold and should comprise at least a small portion of every investment strategy.

3. Growth Investing

This investment strategy focuses on capital appreciation by looking for companies that exhibit signs of above-average growth, even if the share price appears expensive in terms of metrics. This strategy is somewhat riskier and involves investing in smaller companies that have a large potential for growth in growth sectors.

4. Small Cap/Micro Cap Investing

This is for those looking to take on a little more risk in their portfolio. As the name gives away, a small-cap investor focuses on purchasing stocks from small companies who are relatively unknown and thus less expensive. Often referred to as "Penny Stocks", they are companies with very cheap prices that the investor feels are poised to grow exponentially. Bigger companies can have inflated prices since everyone's paying attention to them, while small-cap stocks tend to have fewer people that even know about them. Less risky investors stay away from them due to the risk and most group investors (mutual funds) have restrictions when it comes to investing in them. They are more volatile and therefore difficult to trade.

Whatever you decide, just remember that your goal is a balanced approach with an initial emphasis on Growth Stocks and Investing until you learn the ropes. Then you can enter into more difficult strategies. A balanced investment strategy aims to be more middle of the road and tends to meet the needs of most investors. Its goal is to balance your risk with return and seeks to create a portfolio you are comfortable with.

For example, ask yourself the following when choosing a strategy:

1. Are you wanting to preserve your capital/initial investment?

2. Do you want aggressive or fast returns?

3. Do you want steady income?

4. How long are you willing to let the money remain invested?

Even a balanced investment strategy can be rather aggressive in nature for some and is more suitable for those investors with at least five years to wait for returns. It is very appropriate for a younger investor, who has many more years to work and retirement is a distant goal. If you have a much shorter time frame in mind or a different type of goal that will occur in less than five years, a big purchase (home or vehicle) for instance, you may want to concentrate on a more conservative strategy and focus on the preservation of capital.

Preservation of capital focuses on maintaining current capital levels and preventing/limiting loss. This strategy works mainly with short term and secure investments like government bonds or Certificate of Deposits. A capital preservation strategy will work for older investors or those needing their money for a life event in less than five years. It is for those looking to maximize their current financial assets and to avoid taking significant risks with their chunk of money.

If you are young or have 10 plus years or more to play with a chunk of money you may want to consider an aggressive strategy that maximizes growth, while not concentrating too much on risk. These type of strategy would focus on a portfolio that centers on small-cap stocks, corporate bonds, junk bonds (below investment grade), FOREX (world currencies), real estate, and cryptocurrency. In general, a capital growth portfolio will contain majority stocks and bonds with a smaller amount in currency/real estate and the final bit in cash or even precious metals. Growth-oriented strategies seek high returns by definition, the mixture still protects the investor somewhat from losses on a larger scale while not concentrating too much on a small daily loss.

Why Growth Stocks to Start?

Well from the research we have done it is clear that as a new investor you want to cut your teeth on the simplest type of investment which, for someone with more than 5 years to play with, is Growth Investing. It requires the least amount of research and can yield the greatest returns over time. In fact, a simple Google Search can tell you what companies fall into this category. Simply Google:

1. Growth Industries

2. Best Stocks in the Industry

3. That company's income statements

Remember a growth stock is a share in a company that has shown faster or greater than average growth and has the potential to continue growing faster than the overall economy. The one drawback of these stocks is that because such stocks generally increase in price quicker and in a higher percentage than other stocks, they cost an average of 25% more per share than a value stock. The rapid growth is usually based on the company's current earnings and projected growth over the next 5 to 10 years. In the long run, the price you would pay for the stock is usually justified, but they also tend to be considered a riskier investment.

If a company shows stability or growth over the past 5 years, it is definitely a growth stock, but to make things easier I have compiled a detailed list of the top 100 growth stocks and how they stand at the time of publication in the next section of the book. Read on for the in-depth information.

Stephen Satoshi

Chapter Four Growth Stocks Part 1

Baidu (NASDAQ: BIDU)

Price at time of writing: $165.72 USD

Often dubbed the "Google of China", the Chinese search engine and online advertising leader suffered a 32% dip in 2018, but now looks like the share price has finally reached the bottom.

Chinese ad spending increased 25% year on year, and Baidu still controls roughly 70% of the online advertising space. This isn't showing any signs of slowing down either. In addition to this, the company is investing heavily in Internet of Things (IoT) technology and cloud computing, two more growth markets.

Financials are solid and third quarter sales increased by 27% on a year-on-year period.

Baidu's hidden gem is its strong relationship with the Chinese government. This is vital for any China-based stock as centralization still heavily dominates the business scene.

The big risk here is that Google makes a play to re-enter the Chinese market, which could signal the end of Baidu as the consensus number one. However, Google has tried and failed before to dominate the world's largest country.

This stock isn't for everyone, with any Chinese based stock, you must be willing to bear more volatility, but if there's a space in your portfolio for a potentially explosive growth play, Baidu is a great option.

Horizon Pharma (NASDAQ: HZNP)

Price at time of writing: $24.88 USD

Founded in 2005, this Irish Based Pharma Company in Dublin, Ireland was relocated to Chicago, IL USA. Its specialization was and remains pain and anti-inflammatory remedies.

97% of the company's sales are to US medical companies and doctors, hence the move to the states to save on shipping costs.

Current sales stand at $1.056 billion per year with the vast majority coming from outside

Ireland and the European Area.

Horizon's strengths are in its strong relationship with the USA and North American Market and its recent acquisitions of smaller Pharma companies (Raptor & Hyperion) with their patented Arthritis drugs, Procysbi and Quinsar. This gives them a substantial share in the pain management sector.

The main risks are the large amount of publicity related to the opioid crisis and the loss of patents, but as it stands it is poised for growth in the next 5 to 10 years.

This stock will remain fairly stable even in a downturn so it is appropriate for all investors.

Okta (NASDAQ: OKTA)

Price at time of writing: $99.73 USD

Founded in 1978 in the Balkan Country of Macedonia. Okta is part of the Hellenic Petroleum Group and is one of the biggest providers of fossil-based fuels and cloud software which helps companies manage and secure user authentication into modern applications in the world.

Current sales stand at $7.80 billion per year with product distribution all over the world, especially in Europe.

OTKA's strength is in its strong relationship with the Greek Government. Indeed, this company was owned by the government up until recently when they began transitioning to a private firm.

The main risk is the large amount of attention given to switching away from fossil fuel dependency and onto renewable sources of fuel. However, its other emphasis on cloud technologies will keep it solid.

This stock will remain fairly stable even in a downturn as it provides essential services and is beginning to look at green fuels production.

The fact it is linked to volatile Balkan areas may yield dips and rises more than the average investor would like, but overall it is appropriate for the long hold investor.

W.W. Grainger (NASDAQ: GWW)

Price at time of writing: $292.74 USD

Founded in 1927 in Chicago, IL this company is one of the largest suppliers of industrial supplies to factories, retailers, and construction sites. They currently have over 900 US locations and almost 100 Canadian.

Current sales stand at $10.4 billion with distribution all over the world, the majority of which remains within North America.

Its strengths are in its great reputation and history of stellar service, as well as relationships with the majority of retailers and big construction companies.

The main risks are the large stakes it has in commercial construction which slow during a downturn, but it has a healthy enough maker share with governments and retail that it has remained strong during both a depression and recession.

This stock will remain fairly stable even in a downturn as it provides essential services/products.

The fact it is linked to essential service and has a longstanding history makes it an appropriate stock for most growth investors.

West Pharmaceutical Services (NASDAQ: WST)

Price at time of writing: $115.55 USD

Founded in 1923 in Exton, PA, West Pharmaceutical Services is a designer and manufacturer of pharmaceutical packaging and delivery systems. It is one of the USA's largest producers and designers of prescription/OTC medicines and medical devices, as well as medicinal distribution and delivery of drugs.

Current sales stand at $1.7 billion per year with distribution all over the world.

Its strengths are in its strong ties to American medical companies and providers and the fact that its products are some of the most essential services. An additional strength is its great distribution chain serving Europe and the Far East, as well as North America.

It maintains average risk with the expiration of patents, but West remains a strong company for the future.

This stock will remain fairly stable even in a downturn as it provides essential services.

The fact it is linked to very stable areas will make it a good investment for most investors.

Alibaba (NASDAQ: BABA)

Price at time of writing: $187.37 USD

Founded in 1919 in the Alibaba Group at Xixi in Hangzhou, China, Alibaba is a Chinese multinational conglomerate specializing in e-commerce, retail, internet, and technology. It is one of China's largest consumer, electronics, retail, and payment providers. Think of it as the Amazon/PayPal of China.

Current sales stand at $250 Billion per year with distribution all over the world.

Its strengths are in its strong ties the Chinese Government and the fact its products make up the majority of Far East consumer products and electronic payments. Another significant strength is its great distribution chain serving the Far East

It maintains average risk despite the emerging competition in the space due to its strong sales topping Walmart, eBay, and Amazon Combined in 2015. This stock will remain fairly stable even in a downturn. Also, complaints from Western companies about substandard products will limit exposure in the West.

The fact it is linked to high sales and has a sort of monopoly in this location makes it a good fit for most investors that do not mind the volatility of the Far East.

PayPal (NASDAQ: PYPL)

Price at time of writing: $106.93 USD

Founded in 1998 in Silicon Valley, CA. It started as a subsidiary of eBay to process its payments. It became a universal payment process as an independent company in 2014.

Current sales stand at $13.9 Billion per year with users all over the world.

Its strengths are in its strong ties to the major online retailers with which it works. With online transactions making up over 70% of all transactions. In addition to online dominance, PayPal has negotiated contracts with traditional retailers and individuals for payment for service. It is a top five method of payment all over the world.

It maintains average risk with the emerging competition with retailers and individuals. PayPal continues to expand where it is taken by purchasing European payment processors like IZettle. This stock will remain fairly stable even in a downturn as money transfer is essential.

The fact it is linked to high sales and has a sort of monopoly on payment options allows it to remain strong and ideal for all investors.

Amazon (NASDAQ: AMZN)

Price at time of writing: $1927.39 USD

Founded in 1994 in Seattle, WA Amazon is a technology company that focuses on e-commerce, payment processing, cloud computing, and artificial intelligence. Amazon is the largest e-commerce marketplace and cloud computing platform in the world as measured by revenue and market capitalization. They started as a small online bookseller, but eventually expanded to become the go-to online retailer selling most consumer products and electronics. In the later 2000's it expanded into Fresh Grocery delivery by acquiring Whole Foods, AI with Alexia, and credit by partnering with several banks for credit cards, as well as expanding into Video Streaming/Production and on-demand delivery with Prime and Prime Now.

Current sales stand at $233 billion per year and climbing with users all over the world. It is by far the world's biggest retailer and shows no signs of slowing down. The main drawback is the recent allegations about employee abuse and employment violations. This seems to have been lingering for a number of years, but has died down a bit and has not caused any dip in business.

Its strengths are in its strong ties to multiple industries and its reputation as a bargain place to shop with free delivery.

It maintains average risk with the emerging competition with other retailers and tech companies. This stock will remain fairly stable even in a downturn as it sells many essentials and will be on the front lines of Finance, AI, and Cloud Computing.

The fact that it is linked to high sales and has a partial monopoly on sales allows it to remain strong and ideal for all investors.

Carvana (NASDAQ: CVNA)

Price at time of writing: $67.05 USD

Founded in 2013 in Tempe, AZ as a subsidiary of DriveTime, Carvana became independent in 2014. It started as an online car and parts retailer, but eventually expanded to become a one-stop shop for used vehicles. It is a unique experience that allows shoppers to order, customize, and finance a car for delivery or purchase from their vehicle vending machines at their physical locations.

Current sales stand at $20 million per year and climbing with online and store sales.

Its strengths are in its unique experience as an online car superstore and its vending machine option is a huge attraction if only for the novelty.

It maintains average risk with the emerging competition with other retailers and tech companies. However, this stock will remain fairly stable even in a downturn as it sells cars for rock bottom prices.

The fact that it is a low price leader will keep this a stable stock for most investors.

TriNet Group (NASDAQ: TNET)

Price at time of writing: $62.37 USD

Founded in 1988 in San Leandro, CA as a payroll provider but later expanded to become a one-stop shop for all things payroll and HR, TriNet provides important tasks for small to medium-sized companies that would normally be handled by an in-house employee for a lot less money.

Current sales stand at $3.5 billion per year and climbing as more companies outsource this type of work.

Its strengths are in its reputation and the statistics that say over 75% of companies outsource HR and payroll.

It maintains average risk with the emerging competition with other companies, but the fact it has a longstanding reputation with many established companies are in its favor.

The fact that it is an industry leader will keep this a stable stock for most investors.

Canopy Growth Corp (NASDAQ: CGC)

Price at time of writing: $47.73 USD

Canopy Growth Corp was formerly Tweed Marijuana Inc. and is a cannabis company based in Smiths Falls, Ontario. Tweed was founded by Bruce Linton and Chuck Rifici in 2013 and renamed Canopy Growth Corporation in 2015. Since its inception in 2013, the company has remained in Ontario, Canada as one of a handful of Cannabis Companies present at the time. Canopy Growth Corp still owns over 30% of the market share.

Current sales stand at $40 million per year and climbing as the Cannabis industry expands at a rapid rate.

Its strengths are in its reputation and the fact that it was one for the first legalized producers.

It maintains average risk despite the emerging competition with other companies, especially since many countries and states still have not legalized cannabis yet. CGC remains poised as a leader as any competition will take many years to get established.

The fact it is an industry leader will keep this a stable stock for most that have no moral conflicts with investing in marijuana.

Square (NASDAQ: SQ)

Price at time of writing: $72.46 USD

Founded in 2009 in San Francisco, CA as one of less than 5 point of sale services for individuals and small businesses. Its square reader accepts credit card payments by connecting to a mobile device's audio jack. The original version consisted of a simple read head directly wired to a 3.5 mm audio jack but has expanded into having its own range of full Point of Sale units for businesses.

Current sales stand at $4.5 billion per year and climbing as the premier payment processor of small business and individual proprietors. Its strengths are in its reputation and the fact that it has become synonymous with taking payments- "we've got a square".

It maintains average risk with the emerging competition with other companies, and the fact remains that it is poised as a leader and any others have to play catch up at this point.

The fact it is an industry leader will keep this a stable stock for most investors and it has the potential to go as high as the tech sector.

Control4 (NASDAQ: CTRL)

Price at time of writing: $17.45 USD

Founded in 2003 in Draper, UT, Control4 is a leading global provider of automation, AI, surveillance, and networking for homes and businesses. It offers personalized control of lighting, music, video, comfort, security, and communications integrated into a unified smart home system that enhances the daily lives of its consumers by allowing them to control all aspects of their home from their table, computer, or smartphone. Its main product functions as a creator and designer of automation and networking systems for homes and businesses. It literally joins the multiple networks of single buildings together to allow its residents to do everything seamlessly and without extra effort or the click of a button remotely.

Current sales stand at $15.5 billion per year and climbing as the premier provider of "smart building technology". Its focus is on both on its products and infrastructure.

It maintains average risk with the emerging competition with other companies, but the fact remains that it is poised as a leader and any others have to play catch up at this point.

The fact it is an industry leader will keep this a stable stock for most investors and it has the potential to go as high as the AI sector.

Voyager Therapeutics (NASDAQ: VYGR)

Price at time of writing: $20.75 USD

Voyager Therapeutics is developing life-changing gene therapies focused on severe neurological diseases. Diseases like Parkinson's disease, Huntington's disease, Alzheimer's disease, and other neurodegenerative diseases. They were founded in 2000 by a group of neuroscientists and researchers.

Current sales stand at $12 billion per year and climbing one of the leaders in the biotech field.

Its strengths are in relationships with some of the foremost research facilities in the world.

It maintains low to average risk with the emerging competition with other companies, but the fact remains that it is still the definitive leader in the neurological area and any others have lots of research to do to catch up.

The fact it is an industry leader will keep this a stable stock for most investors and it has the potential to go as high as the tech sector.

Kinross Gold (NASDAQ: KGC)

Price at time of writing: $3.15 USD

Founded in 1993 in Toronto Ontario, Canada as one the best miners of gold and silver in North America. It currently operates eight active gold mines and was ranked fourth of the "10 Top Gold-mining Companies" of 2017 by several business publications.

Current sales stand at $3.3 million per year and climbing as one of the last full-scale extractors of precious metals. The gold and silver industries have remained stable and Kinross will continue to be one of the only players in town to do the job.

It maintains above average risk with the shrinkage of the mining industry in general, but as one of less than a handful of players, it will keep its market share. The very cheap price is one that should be bought in bulk while the price is low.

The fact it is an industry leader will keep this a stable stock for most investors and it has the potential.

Mitsubishi (NASDAQ: MSBHY)

Price at time of writing: $54.57 USD

Founded in 1871 as a manufacturer of Japanese Steamboats, no company on this list is older than Mitsubishi, it has been through several alterations and evolutions during its long history. From steamboats to insurance and then to weapons for the Japanese War effort, before it was finally revamped as a car manufacturer in the 1950s. It still remains very diverse today and is on the cutting edge of all its industries. It is the sixth-largest Japanese automaker and the nineteenth-largest worldwide by production standards. Since 2016, Mitsubishi has been almost one-third (34%) owned by Nissan and is now a part of the Renault–Nissan–Mitsubishi Alliance.

Current sales stand at $552 billion per year and climbing as its flexes it muscles across all of the following by focusing on various sectors within its industry. Some of its work includes computer/processing technology, transportation, water, electricity and industrial projects; asset management, asset financing, real estate and logistics; investment in all forms of energy including fossil fuels and renewable energy; precious metals and industrial raw ingredients; manufacturing of many types of vehicles including cars and military; and consumer products.

Its strengths are in its diversification and solid reputation across all its sectors.

It maintains low risk with the emerging competition with other companies, and the fact remains that it is hard to compete with based on size alone.

The fact it is an industry leader will keep this a stable stock for most investors and it has the potential to go as high as any of its sectors.

Vanda Pharmaceuticals (NASDAQ: VNDA)

Price at time of writing: $17.31 USD

Founded in 1999 in Germany as one of the few leaders in what are considered unmet medical needs in the areas of sleep deprivation and schizophrenia. Its drugs for these ailments are its premier products.

Current sales stand at $225 million per year and climbing as much as 17% year by year as the number one producer of mental health medicines related to mood and sleep.

It maintains low risk with the emerging competition with other companies, as few show any interest competing for its niche market share.

The fact it is an industry leader will keep this a stable stock for most investors and it has the potential to go as high as the biotech sector.

XPO Logistics (NASDAQ: XPO)

Price at time of writing: $67.05 USD

Founded in 1989 in Greenwich CE as a simple trucking company. Today XPO logistics operates in 32 countries and is the preferred logistics company for 67 of the Forbes Fortune 100 companies. It is one of the world's 10 largest providers of transportation and logistics services. XPO operates as a third-party provider in over 25 countries and has over 35,000 customers, including 70 of the Fortune 100.

Current sales stand at $17 billion per year and climbing as the premier delivery and freight company of the elites of business. It is also heavily investing in the future by working with Tesla to test the autonomous trucks and with other AI companies for Smart Distribution Centers, so it is poised for the future.

It maintains average risk with the emerging competition with other companies, but the fact remains that it is poised as a leader with deep connections to those that need their services.

The fact it is an industry leader will keep this a stable stock for most investors and it has the potential to go as high as the logistics sector.

HubSpot (NASDAQ: HUBS)

Price at time of writing: $166.23 USD

Founded in 2005 at MIT in Boston, HubSpot remains a leader in software and cloud computing solutions for social media and online advertising in general.

Current sales stand at $553 million per year and climbing as the supplier of advertising products on Facebook, Instagram, and Twitter. This is in addition to the software it provided for SEO optimization and Adwords Searches.

It maintains average risk with the emerging competition with other companies, there are very few that can turn out the number of quality products and establish the partnership with Google and Facebook that HubSpot already has.

The fact it is an industry leader will keep this a stable stock for most investors and it has the potential to go as high as the tech sector.

Veeva Systems (NASDAQ: VEEV)

Price at time of writing: $136.57 USD

Founded in 2007 in Pleasanton, CA. It is one of the few in the burgeoning industry crossover of biotech and cloud computing. It develops and services software that aids in cutting edge life science research across the globe.

Current sales stand at $100 billion per year and climbing as the premier supplier and creator of software that organizes and services the top researchers in the life, environmental, and medical fields.

It maintains low risk as emerging competition is low in the niche, and the fact remains that it is poised as a leader and any others have to play catch up at this point.

The fact it is an industry leader will keep this a stable stock for most investors and it has the potential to go as high as the tech sector.

Adobe (NASDAQ: ADBE)

Price at time of writing: $278.49 USD

Founded in 1982 in San Jose, CA as a creative software company. Adobe primarily focuses on the creation of multimedia and creativity software products, with a more recent foray towards digital marketing software.

Current sales stand at $9.3 billion per year and climbing as the premier creator and marketer of creative and not marketing software.

It maintains low risk despite the emerging competition with other companies due to the solid grip it has on the industry.

The fact it is an industry leader will keep this a stable stock for most investors and it has the potential to go as high as the tech sector.

Cerner Corp. (NASDAQ: CERN)

Price at time of writing: $63.83 USD

Founded in 1979 in Kansas City, MO as a provider of healthcare IT (HIT) software, hardware, and medical devices. Cerner Corporation is a supplier of health information technology solutions, services, devices, and hardware. Its products are in use at more than 25,000 facilities around the world. The company has more than 30,000 employees globally, with over 12,000 in its HQ in Kansas City, Missouri.

Current sales stand at $5.3 billion per year and climbing as the premier provider of HIT-related gadgets and tools to the vast majority of US and European Medical Companies.

It maintains low risk despite the emerging competition as it is generally well connected with the decision makers in the medical industry and provides stellar service and quality.

The fact it is an industry leader will keep this a stable stock for most investors and it has the potential to go as high as the bio sector.

Salesforce (NASDAQ: CRM)

Price at time of writing: $161.23 USD

Founded in 1999 in San Francisco, CA as a provider of client management and scheduling software. It has expanded to a 95% cloud-based system that primarily works with sales and service companies in the realm of client management and sales tracking. Its main product is a cloud computing service as a software (SaaS) company that specializes in customer relationship management (CRM). The software is number one for customer success and helps businesses track customer activity, sales, revenues, market to customers, and many more elements involved in customer management.

Current sales stand at $10.48 billion per year and climbing as the premier provider of sales and client tracking software and cloud-based systems. It also provides analytics, customer service, and data tracking software.

It maintains low risk despite the emerging competition in this sector as many are trying to break in this wide open niche. However, the fact remains that it is poised as a leader and any others have to play catch up at this point.

The fact it is an industry leader will keep this a stable stock for most investors and it has the potential to go as high as the tech sector.

CSX Corp. (NASDAQ: CSX)

Price at time of writing: $79.02 USD

Founded in 1980 in Jacksonville FL as a provider of rail and railroad equipment for the vast train logistics chains across the USA. Presently it has expanded into heavy equipment for industrial use and real estate holdings.

Current sales stand at $5.4 billion per year and climbing as the provider for the railroad industry and industrial real estate.

It maintains low risk with very little competition in its areas of interest and is poised for a bright future in the industry. It has invested in smart warehouse and smart car technologies that will make it the forerunner for the future of the mass transit sector.

The fact it is an industry leader will keep this a stable stock for most investors and it has the potential to go as high as the logistics sector.

Activision Blizzard (NASDAQ: ATVI)

Price at time of writing: $46.51 USD

Activision was founded in 2008 in Santa Monica, CA as a producer of film, video, and video games. Among its most popular titles are Treyarch, Infinity Ward, High Moon Studios and Toys for Bob, Call of Duty, Guitar Hero, Tony Hawk's, and Spyro/Skylanders through Activision's studios, as well as World of Warcraft, StarCraft, Diablo, Candy Crush Saga, Hearthstone, and Overwatch.

Current sales stand at $7.5 billion per year and climbing as Activision continues to release new games and update the most popular ones with new releases. In 2018, its release of Call of Duty: Black Ops 4 and its re-release of the popular game is Candy Crush Saga are just a few examples of successful new games.

It maintains average risk with the emerging competition with other companies, but the fact remains that it is the creator of some of the most popular titles in the history of gaming and it will remain a leader in the industry. The only wild card is the recently proposed regulations on the practice of microtransactions both in free games and purchased games. Within the realm of free games (like Activision's Candy Crush or Hearthstone) players are charged a few cents for advanced tactics, weapons, or tools. It is generally the only way these games make money, but the problem is that the practice has extended to paid games. This happens when you are charged money in game for more weapons/updates/designs. This resulted in many complaints and bills are being proposed to limit this. We predict no big issues, but it is something to watch.

The fact it is an industry leader will keep this a stable stock for most investors and it has the potential to go as high as the tech sector.

Expedia Group (NASDAQ: EXPE)

Price at time of writing: $125.88 USD

Founded in 1996 in Bellevue, WA as a part of Microsoft, Expedia is currently one of the largest providers of travel software and booking platforms in the world. It owns the well-known names of Hotels.com, Expedia, Travelocity, CarRentals.com, CheapTickets, HomeAway, Hotwire.com, Orbitz, Travelocity, Trivago, and Venere.com.

Current sales stand at $10.5 billion per year and climbing as the provider of the most travel booking services in the world. It has partnerships with many airlines, hotels, car rentals companies, and other leisure providers. It has the strength of exclusive cheap pricing and an excellent reputation for service.

It maintains a very low risk with the emerging competition as there is very little of it, as Expedia has the partnerships to remain the industry leader. In short, Expedia competes only with itself in this industry.

The fact it is an industry leader will keep this a stable stock for most investors and it has the potential to go as high as the tech and travel sector.

Chapter Five Growth Stocks Part 2

Emerson Electric (NASDAQ: EMR)

Price at time of writing: $73.16 USD

Founded in 1890 and currently residing in Ferguson, MO (outside St. Louis), Emerson Electric is a provider of engineering services to major manufacturers and utilities across the USA.

Current sales stand at $15.6 billion per year and climbing as the premier provider of engineering, maintenance, and support services to public utilities and manufacturers.

It maintains low risk with very little competition in the area and is poised for a bright future in the industry. Its strong relationships with many essential service providers make it strong even in a downturn.

The fact that it is an industry leader will keep this a stable stock for most investors and it has the potential to go as high as the logistics/engineering sector.

Wynn Resorts (NASDAQ: WYNN)

Price at time of writing: $143.44 USD

Founded in 2002 and currently residing in Los Vegas, NV, Wynn Resorts is a provider of gambling, entertainment, and leisure across many properties in the Western and Eastern portions of the USA. One of its major properties opened during the 2006 recession and maintained decent profits, so they are in it for the long haul.

Current sales stand at $4.4 billion per year and climbing as the premier provider of leisure services.

It maintains low risk due to the strong ties to state gaming commissions and Native American Tribes that manage many of its properties. Its strong relationship with the aforementioned entities allows it to remain strong even in a downturn.

The fact it is an industry leader will keep this a stable stock for most investors and it has the potential to go as high as the gaming sector.

Crocs (NASDAQ: CROX)

Price at time of writing: $26.85 USD

Founded in 2002 and currently residing in Boulder, CO, Crocs is a provider of footwear and apparel for men, women, and children. Originally founded to make light foam shoes for boaters and fishermen.

Current sales stand at $1 billion per year and climbing as the brand has caught on with the general public and has found their way into the pop culture.

It maintains low risk with very little competition within its niche and is poised for a bright future in the industry. Its strong relationships with many huge retailers and brand loyalty from its wearers confer strength to its position in the market.

The fact it is an industry leader will keep this a stable stock for most investors and it has the potential to go as high as the clothing sector.

Twilio (NASDAQ: TWLO)

Price at time of writing: $130.23 USD

Founded in 2008 and currently residing in San Francisco, CA, Twilio is a provider of web-based communication to businesses and allows the use of its APIs to complete a variety of communications like texts/calls via their databases. It is very comparable to Slack and Skype and has excelled in partnering with other top companies such as LuLulemon. Twilio supports the development of open-source software and regularly makes contributions to the open-source community. They recently launched OpenVBX, an open-source product that lets business users configure phone numbers to receive and route phone calls. It also sponsors Localtunnel which enables software developers to expose their local development environment to the public internet. The fact that it supports open source makes it a darling of the tech world.

Current sales stand at $650 million per year and climbing as the premier provider of these services to major companies and government entities.

It maintains low risk with very little competition in the area and is poised for a bright future in the industry. Its strong relationships with many large companies and its cutting edge research to improve its communication system are key to keeping it strong.

The fact it is an industry leader will keep this a stable stock for most investors and it has the potential to go as high as the tech sector.

LuLulemon (NASDAQ: LULU)

Price at time of writing: $176.17 USD

Founded in 1998 and currently residing in Vancouver BC, Canada, Lululemon is a provider of athletic apparel for women and men. It has evolved from an athletic brand into a designer brand known for comfort, style, and quality.

Current sales stand at $2.6 billion per year and climbing as it has become a high fashion brand with a thriving resale market online.

It maintains low risk with very little competition as its resellers and those that wear it are fiercely loyal. In addition, the fact that a garment can last years, even under high use makes it a good fit for those looking to get the most for their money.

The fact it is an industry leader will keep this a stable stock for most investors and it has the potential to go as high as the designer/athletic clothing sectors.

MongoDB (NASDAQ: MDB)

Price at time of writing: $136.97 USD

Founded in 2007 and currently residing in NY, NY, MongoDB is a provider of database management services in a cloud environment to millions of users. It allows businesses to manage their own database of information, without having to maintain servers and other bulky items.

Current sales stand at $25 billion per year and climbing as the premier provider of data management for a host of retailers, companies, and small businesses.

It maintains low risk with very little competition in the area and is poised for a bright future in the industry. Its strong relationships with many businesses and stellar track record for service and research will keep it strong.

The fact it is an industry leader will keep this a stable stock for most investors and it has the potential to go as high as the logistics/engineering sector.

Sarepta Therapeutics (NASDAQ: SRPT)

Price at time of writing: $116.86 USD

Founded in 1980 in Cambridge, MA, Sarepta Therapeutics is a provider of research and pharmaceuticals geared toward anti-viral treatments and respiratory ailments. Some of its major products are known for treating West Nile Virus, Hepatitis, and Pneumonia.

Current sales stand at $5.5 billion per year and climbing as the premier provider of these drugs to hospitals, clinics, and medical professionals.

It maintains low risk with he very little competition in the area and is poised for a bright future in the industry. Its strong reputation with respiratory and viral research will make it a leader for many years.

The fact it is an industry leader will keep this a stable stock for most investors and it has the potential to go as high as the biotech sector.

Netflix (NASDAQ: NFLX)

Price at time of writing: $377.23 USD

Founded in 1997 in Los Gatos, CA, Netflix began with mail-order DVD rentals and has since morphed into the leader in digital streaming and a provider of original movies and programming.

Current sales stand at $15.7 billion per year and climbing as the premier provider of these services worldwide. Recently released financial statements show consistent growth from month to month, indicating that its business model is effective.

It maintains low risk with very little competition in the niche of the one-stop streaming shop and an independent studio. The only other platforms close are HULU and AMAZON, but the former's ties to cable TV and the latter's emphasis on retail rather than streaming makes Netflix the clear winner. Netflix is poised for a bright future in the industry. Its strong relationship with many large companies and its cutting edge research to improve its communication system are key to keeping it strong.

The fact it is an industry leader will keep this a stable stock for most investors and it has the potential to go as high as the tech sector.

Qualcomm (NASDAQ: QCOM)

Price at time of writing: $88.10 USD

Founded in 1985 in San Diego, CA, Qualcomm is a provider of semiconductor and wireless communications equipment worldwide. They provide the guts that make the wireless data market work such as towers, antennas, and fiber optics.

Current sales stand at $22.7 billion per year and climbing as the premier provider of these services to major companies and government entities.

It maintains low risk with very little competition in the area and is poised for a bright future in the industry. Its strong relationship with many large companies and its cutting edge research to improve its systems and keep up with every generation of wireless data are fundamental to its strong position in the industry.

The fact it is an industry leader will keep this a stable stock for most investors and it has the potential to go as high as the tech sector.

Alphabet Inc. (NASDAQ: GOOGLE)

Price at time of writing: $12733.88 USD

Founded in 2015 and currently residing in Mountain View, CA, Alphabet Inc. is the parent company of Google which is the number one search engine in the world. In addition, they own

YouTube the 2nd largest search engine, as well as being the go-to company for advertising, research, and AI.

Current sales stand at $136 billion per year and climbing as the premier provider of these services to major companies, individuals, and government entities.

It maintains low risk with very little competition in the area and is poised for a bright future in the industry. Its strong relationship with many large companies and its cutting edge research to improve its market reach is key to keeping it strong.

The fact it is an industry leader will keep this a stable stock for most investors and it has the potential to go as high as the tech sector.

iRobot (NASDAQ: IRBT)

Price at time of writing: $103.36 USD

Founded in 1990 by 3 MIT students in Cambridge, MA and currently residing in Bedford, MA, iRobot is a provider of AI-based home products like the Roomba. It is also developing a line of police, fire protection, and military robots. It has an exclusive agreement with the military for battle robots and is the largest provider of personal robots in the world, the most commonly known of which is the Roomba.

Current sales stand at $1.79 billion per year and climbing as the premier provider of these products to the military and individuals.

It maintains low risk with very little competition in the area of homes based AI gadgets and is poised for a bright future in the industry. Its strong relationship with many large retailers and its cutting edge research to improve its products and expand its offerings into the new sector of smart homes will keep iRobot a strong player in the industry.

The fact it is an industry leader will keep this a stable stock for most investors and it has the potential to go as high as the tech and AI sector.

Facebook (NASDAQ: FB)

Price at time of writing: $183.20 USD

Founded in 2004 in Cambridge MA by four Harvard Students and currently residing in Silicon Valley, CA, Facebook provides the largest social media platform in the world with 40 billion active users. It also provides one of the largest advertising and marketing platforms in the world between FB and its acquisition of Instagram.

Current sales stand at $56 billion per year and climbing as the premier provider of these services to major companies, individuals and government entities. Its recently released balance sheets show consistent growth, indicating that it has a strong business model.

It maintains low risk with very little competition in the area and is poised for a bright future in the industry. Its strong relationship with many large companies and its cutting edge research to improve its platform is key to keeping it strong.

The fact it is an industry leader will keep this a stable stock for most investors and it has the potential to go as high as the tech sector.

JD.com (NASDAQ: JD)

Price at time of writing: $29.50 USD

Founded in 1998 and currently residing in Beijing China, JD.com is a provider of e-commerce and consumer products in China and the Far East.

Current sales stand at $65 billion per year and climbing as the premier provider of these services to the areas around China.

It maintains low risk with very little competition in the area and is poised for a bright future in the industry. Its strong relationships with many local governments and its cutting edge research to improve its operations are key to keeping it strong.

The fact it is an industry leader will keep this a stable stock for some investors (that are not bothered by the volatility of China) and it has the potential to go as high as the tech sector.

Shake Shack (NASDAQ: SHAK)

Price at time of writing: $61.25 USD

Founded in 2004 and currently residing in New York, NY, Shake Shack is a provider of fast-casual food and shakes in a clean and inexpensive environment. It started as a simple hot dog cart and has grown to a chain with 200 locations in both the US and foreign countries.

Current sales stand at $650 million per year and climbing as a premier provider of American style food in a quick clean environment. They are a few steps above typical fast food and have better service and ingredients. Think Chipotle for American style food.

It maintains low risk with very little competition in the area of fast casual burgers/shakes and is poised for a bright future in the industry. Its strong reputation and fast expansion within the niche system is key to keeping it strong.

The fact it is an industry leader will keep this a stable stock for most investors and it has the potential to go as high as the food sector.

Tesla (NASDAQ: TSLA)

Price at time of writing: $263.33 USD

Founded in 2003 and currently residing in Palo Alto, CA, Tesla is the premier provider of renewable energy and electric cars to the USA and the world. In fact, they have done so well that when one thinks of an electric car, they think Tesla.

Current sales stand at $21.4 billion per year and climbing as the premier provider of these services to major companies, individuals, and government entities.

It maintains low risk with very little competition in the area and is poised for a bright future in the industry. Its strong relationship with many large companies and its cutting edge research to improve its products is key to keeping it strong.

The fact it is an industry leader will keep this a stable stock for most investors and it has the potential to go as high as the tech sector.

Nike (NASDAQ: NKE)

Price at time of writing: $88.50 USD

Founded in 1964 and currently residing in Beaverton, OR, Nike is a provider of athletic equipment, apparel, and shoes for individuals, teams, and companies. One of the largest in the niche with exclusive contracts with many of the professional, high school, and college sports teams and leagues. Its revenues continue to climb year after year as evident in their recently released financial statements, which can be found on their website.

Current sales stand at $36 billion per year and climbing as the premier provider of these services and products.

It maintains low risk with very little competition in the area and is poised for a bright future in the industry. Its strong relationship with many large companies, sports leagues, and colleges and its cutting edge research to improve products will keep it strong.

The fact it is an industry leader will keep this a stable stock for most investors and it has the potential to go as high as the sports sector.

Boeing (NASDAQ: BA)

Price at time of writing: $376.76 USD

Founded in 1916 in Seattle, WA and currently residing in Chicago, IL, Boeing is a provider of aircraft, weapons, and military equipment for the US government, Allies, and airlines. In addition to providing the Boeing Jet Series, it also has exclusive duties with many government entities for year 2018/2019.

Current sales stand at $102 billion per year and climbing as the premier provider of these services to major companies and government entities. It has contracts with both the USA and its Allies for military equipment.

It maintains low risk with very little competition in the area and is poised for a bright future in the industry. Its strong relationships with the government and large companies and its cutting edge research to improve its products are key to keeping it strong.

The fact that it is an industry leader will keep this a stable stock for most investors and it has the potential to go as high as the tech sector.

Visa (NASDAQ: V)

Price at time of writing: $161.68 USD

Founded in 1958 and currently residing in Foster City, CA, Visa is the number one provider of branded credit, debit, and prepaid charge cards in the world. In addition, it provides payment processing and financial support to many banks and financial institutions.

Current sales stand at $18 billion per year and climbing as the premier provider of these services to major banks, companies, and government entities.

It maintains low risk with very little competition in the area and is poised for a bright future in the industry. Its strong relationship with many large companies and its cutting edge research to improve its communication system is key to keeping it strong.

The fact it is an industry leader will keep this a stable stock for most investors and it has the potential to go as high as the tech and finance sector.

Nokia (NASDAQ: NOK)

Price at time of writing: $5.83 USD

Founded in 1865 and near Helsinki, Finland as a pulp mill, Nokia is currently a provider of web-based communication, wireless communication devices, smart devices, and sell their support system to businesses, schools, and individuals.

Current sales stand at $22.5 billion per year and climbing as one of the premier providers of these services to major companies, individuals, and government entities.

It maintains average risk despite the competition in the area and is poised for a bright future in the industry. Its strong relationship with many large companies and its cutting edge research to improve its communication system is key to keeping it strong.

The fact it is an industry leader will keep this a stable stock for most investors and it has the potential to go as high as the tech sector.

Skyworks Solutions (NASDAQ: SWKS)

Price at time of writing: $89.73 USD

Founded in 2002 and currently residing in Woburn, MA, Skyworks Solutions is a provider of semiconductors, sound adapters, and wireless networking systems for wireless infrastructure.

Current sales stand at $3.2 million per year and climbing as a rising provider of these services to major companies and government entities.

It maintains average risk with the limited competition in the area and is poised for a bright future in the industry. Its strong relationship with many large companies and its cutting edge research to improve its communication system is key to keeping it strong.

The fact it is an industry leader will keep this a stable stock for most investors and it has the potential to go as high as the tech sector.

Samsung (NASDAQ: SSNLF)

Price at time of writing: $44.20 USD

Founded in 1937 and currently residing in Seoul, South Korea, Samsung is a provider of wireless communication devices, smart technology, and is a leader in the research around it.

Current sales stand at $210 billion per year and climbing as the premier provider of these services to major companies and government entities. It stands as the number one provider of wireless equipment, even taking a leading position above Apple.

It maintains low risk even with some prime competition in the sector and is poised for a bright future in the industry. Its strong relationship with many large companies and its cutting edge research to improve its communication system is key to keeping it strong. Also, Samsung has become the go-to company for manufacturers using android based systems and products and will continue to grow within that niche.

The fact it is an industry leader will keep this a stable stock for most investors and it has the potential to go as high as the tech sector.

United Technologies (NASDAQ: UTX)

Price at time of writing: $139.14 USD

Founded in 1934 and currently residing in Farmington, CE, United Technologies is a provider of engines, HVAC components, security systems, elevators/escalators, and other industrial products. It has many subsidiaries, a few of them are shown below as listed on their website.

- Otis Elevator Company: Manufacturer, installer, and servicer of elevators, escalators, and moving walkways.

- Pratt & Whitney: Designs and builds aircraft engines and gas turbines.

- Collins Aerospace: Designs and manufactures aerospace systems for commercial, regional, corporate and military aircraft.

- UTC Climate, Controls & Security: Makes fire detection and suppression systems, access control systems. Conditioning, and refrigeration systems.

- United Technologies Research Center (UTRC): A centralized research facility.

Current sales stand at $66 billion per year and climbing as the premier provider of these services to major companies and government entities. Earnings reports show strong growth, indicating that it is a major player with a successful business model.

It maintains low risk with very little competition in the area and is poised for a bright future in the industry. Its strong relationship with many large companies and its cutting edge research to improve its communication system is key to keeping it strong.

The fact it is an industry leader will keep this a stable stock for most investors and it has the potential to go as high as the logistics sector.

Clorox (NASDAQ: CLX)

Price at time of writing: $153.39 USD

Founded in 1916 and currently residing in Oakland, CA, Clorox is a provider of both chemicals, consumer products, and food products for consumers. It operates under several well-known brands like Burt's Bees and many others.

Current sales stand at $6.1 billion per year and climbing as the premier provider of these products to consumers.

It maintains low risk with very little competition in the area and is poised for a bright future in the industry. Its strong relationships with many large companies and consumer brand loyalty indicate that it will remain a strong player.

The fact it is an industry leader will keep this a stable stock for most investors and it has the potential to go as high as the retail sector.

Duke Energy (NASDAQ: DUK)

Price at time of writing: $89.42 USD

Founded in 1904 and currently residing in Charlotte, NC, Duke Energy is a provider of energy and utilities to many customers across the USA, Canada, and South America. Duke Energy now has many subsidiaries, both in the USA and internationally.

Current sales stand at $22 billion per year and climbing as the premier provider of these services to major utilities and government entities. It operates 10% of the major utilities in the USA.

It maintains low risk with very little competition in the area and is poised for a bright future in the industry. Its strong relationship with many large companies is key to keeping it strong.

The fact it is an industry leader will keep this a stable stock for most investors and it has the potential to go as high as the biotech and utilities sectors.

Chapter Six Growth Stocks Part 3

Realty Income (NASDAQ: O)

Price at time of writing: $69.96 USD

Founded in 1950 and currently residing in San Diego, CA, Realty Income was originally a real estate management company but now is a REIT. This, as you remember from earlier chapters, pools money for investment in real estate and pays dividends based on the profits. This is a rare thing as it is both growth and income stock.

Current sales stand at $1.25 billion per year and climbing as the premier provider of investment in commercial and industrial properties.

It maintains low risk with very little competition in the area and is poised for a bright future in the industry. Its strong relationship with many large companies and the ability to buy larger properties will keep it ahead of the game.

The fact it is an industry leader will keep this a stable stock for most investors and it has the potential to go as high as the real estate sector. Even in a downturn, it will remain stable.

3M (NASDAQ: MMM)

Price at time of writing: $218.52 USD

Founded in 1902 and currently residing in Maplewood, MN, 3M was originally a mining company but now has a huge stake in the consumer product manufacturing, healthcare, security, and marketing sectors.

Current sales stand at $31 billion per year and climbing as the premier provider of these services to individuals. They also have a significant degree of brand loyalty in their manufactured brands. With a strong recent income report published to their website, 3M is set to remain successful.

It maintains low risk with its diversified businesses. Its strong relationship with many large companies and its consumer brand loyalty and reputation will keep it strong.

The fact it is an industry leader will keep this a stable stock for most investors and it has the potential to go as high as the many sectors it works in.

Starbucks (NASDAQ: SBUX)

Price at time of writing: $75.35 USD

Founded in 1971 and currently residing in Seattle, WA, Starbucks is a provider of coffee and cafe items across thousands of locations nationwide and internationally.

Current sales stand at $23 billion per year and climbing as the premier provider of these products to the public through 20,000 stores in 62 countries around the world, and growing.

It maintains low risk even with the competition in the area and is poised for a bright future in the industry. Its strong relationship with many large companies and its cutting edge research to improve its communication system are key to keeping it strong.

The fact it is an industry leader will keep this a stable stock for most investors.

Abbvie (NASDAQ: ABBV)

Price at time of writing: $78.63 USD

Founded in 2013 and currently residing in near Chicago, IL, Abbvie is a provider of cancer drugs and research and is a spinoff of Abbott Labs.

Current sales stand at $32 billion per year and climbing as the premier provider of these drugs.

It maintains low risk with very little competition in the area and is poised for a bright future in the industry. Its strong relationship with many large companies and its cutting edge research to improve current drugs develop new ones is a boon.

The fact it is an industry leader will keep this a stable stock for most investors.

TD Bank (NASDAQ: TD)

Price at time of writing: $55.61 USD

Founded in 1965 and currently residing in Toronto, Canada, TD Bank is Canada's largest bank and financial institution.

Current sales stand at $36 billion per year and climbing as the premier provider of these services to major companies and government entities.

It maintains low risk with very little competition in the area and is poised for a bright future in the industry. Its strong relationship with many large companies and its cutting edge research to improve its communication system is key to keeping it strong.

The fact it is an industry leader will keep this a stable stock for most investors.

Altria (NASDAQ: MO)

Price at time of writing: $54.58 USD

Founded in 1985 and currently residing in Henrico County, VA, Altria is a rebranding of the tobacco company Philip Morris.

Current sales stand at $27 billion per year and climbing as the company revamps to stop the damage of the no-smoking campaign. It is venturing into the e-cig market and exploring areas such as cannabis.

It maintains average risk with very little competition in the area and but is the riskiest of the growth stocks as it must overcome its past. Its strong relationship with many large companies and its cutting edge research to improve and expand its offerings will keep it stable in the future.

The fact it is an industry leader will keep this a stable stock for most investors but due to past industry shifts, it should be watched closely.

International Paper (NASDAQ: IP)

Price at time of writing: $44.63 USD

Founded in 1898 in New York by a merging of 17 paper mills and currently residing in Memphis, TN, International Paper is a provider of paper and paper products to the US government and other governments as well as private companies.

Current sales stand at $21 billion per year and climbing as the premier provider of these services to major companies and government entities. It restructured in 2006 to become much leaner and offset the paperless revolution. It is researching other potentially useful materials like hemp and other alternatives to paper.

It maintains low risk with very little competition in the area and is poised for a bright future in the industry. Its strong relationship with many large companies and its cutting edge research to improve and diversify its products is a pro.

The fact it is an industry leader will keep this a stable stock for most investors. However, it is in a shrinking industry so keep your eye on this one.

Cisco (NASDAQ: CSCO)

Price at time of writing: $56.85 USD

Founded in 1985 and currently residing in San Francisco, CA, Cisco is a provider of web-based services and hardware/software, as well as infrastructure components to enable the use of Wi-Fi and net technologies.

Current sales stand at $46 billion per year and climbing as the premier provider of these services to major companies and government entities. Its growth is demonstrated by its past year's income available on their website.

It maintains low risk with very little competition in the area and is poised for a bright future in the industry. Its strong relationship with many large companies and its cutting edge research to improve its communication system are key to keeping it strong.

The fact it is an industry leader will keep this a stable stock for most investors.

CVS (NASDAQ: CVS)

Price at time of writing: $52.96 USD

Founded in 1996 and currently residing in Woonsocket, RI, CVS is a provider of medical research and pharmacy services to businesses, medical professionals, and individuals

Current sales stand at $184 billion per year and climbing as the premier provider of these services to major companies and the general public. It has consistently grown and has expanded into health clinics and insurance.

It maintains low risk with limited competition in the area and is poised for a bright future in the industry. Its strong relationship with many large companies and its cutting edge research to improve its offerings is key to keeping it strong.

The fact it is an industry leader will keep this a stable stock for most investors.

Walgreens (NASDAQ: WBA)

Price at time of writing: $53.52 USD

Founded in 1901 and currently residing in Chicago, IL, Walgreens is a provider of medical research and pharmacy services to businesses, medical professionals, and individuals

Current sales stand at $183 billion per year and climbing as the premier provider of these services to major companies and government entities as well as the general public.

It maintains low risk with limited competition in the area and is poised for a bright future in the industry. Its strong relationship with many large companies and its cutting edge research to improve its offerings are key to keeping it strong.

The fact it is an industry leader will keep this a stable stock for most investors.

Molson Coors (NASDAQ: TAP)

Price at time of writing: $63.87 USD

Founded in 2005 via a merger between Molson of Canada and Coors Co. and currently residing in Denver, CO, it is a major provider of beer and other alcoholic beverages/consumer products worldwide.

Current sales stand at $4.8 billion per year and climbing as the premier provider of these services to major companies and government entities.

It maintains average risk despite the competition in the sector and is poised for a bright future in the industry. Its strong relationship with many large wholesalers and its cutting brand loyalty and reputation for value will keep it strong.

The fact it is an industry leader will keep this a stable stock for most investors and since beer is usually stable during downturns you don't need to fear a recession.

NXP Semiconductors (NASDAQ: NXPI)

Price at time of writing: $100.49 USD

Founded in 1953 and currently residing in the Netherlands, NXP Semiconductors is a provider of semiconductors and infrastructure components for the wireless industry.

Current sales stand at $9 billion per year and climbing as a premier provider of these services to major companies and government entities around the world.

It maintains low risk with very little competition in the area and is poised for a bright future in the industry. Its strong relationships with many large companies and its cutting edge research to improve its communication system are key to keeping it strong. In addition, it has one of the best supply and distribution chains in the world including China, Thailand, Japan, Europe, and the USA.

The fact it is an industry leader will keep this a stable stock for most investors.

Viacom (NASDAQ: VIA)

Price at time of writing: $36.66 USD

Founded in 2013 and currently residing in NY, NY, Viacom is a worldwide entertainment provider. It was formed by a merger and consolidation between CBS and other media companies.

Current sales stand at $12.5 billion per year and climbing as the premier provider of these services to the world. Its holdings have a foothold in TV and movies and include well-known names such as Paramount and Nickelodeon.

It maintains average risk despite the competition in the area and is poised for a bright future in the industry. Its strong relationship with many large companies and its cutting edge research to improve its communication system are key to keeping it strong.

The fact it is an industry leader will keep this a stable stock for most investors.

Kraft Heinz (NASDAQ: KHC)

Price at time of writing: $32.70 USD

Founded in 2015 and currently residing in Pittsburg, PA and Chicago, IL, the company is a merger of the companies Kraft and Heinz. It is a provider of consumer products and foods.

Current sales stand at $6.5 billion per year and climbing as the premier provider of these products with unrivaled brand loyalty. Its recently published sales chart can be accessed from its website and shows consistent growth each year.

It maintains low risk with very little competition in the area and is poised for a bright future in the industry. Its strong relationship with many large companies and its ever-expanding brand list keeps it an industry leader.

The fact it is an industry leader will keep this a stable stock for most investors.

Tencent (NASDAQ: TCTZF)

Price at time of writing: $49.76 USD

Founded in 1998 and currently residing in China, Tencent is a conglomerate that produces a wide range of technology including AI, wireless products, telecommunications, and consumer products. Some of its well-known products are video games, online payments (Paipal), e-commerce, and the search engine Soso. In addition, they are a Google AdSense partner and run their own social media platform known as TencentQ.

Current sales stand at $300 billion per year and climbing as the premier provider of these services to major companies and Far East government entities.

It maintains low risk with very little competition in the area and is poised for a bright future in the industry. Its strong relationship with many large companies and its cutting edge research to improve its communication system are key to keeping it strong.

Huya (NASDAQ: HUYA)

Price at time of writing: $22.72 USD

Founded in 2008 and currently residing in San Francisco, CA, Huya is a provider of web-based communication to businesses and allows the use of its APIs to perform a variety of communications like texts/calls via their databases.

Current sales stand at $650 million per year and climbing as the premier provider of these services to major companies and government entities.

It maintains low risk with very little competition in the area and is poised for a bright future in the industry. Its strong relationship with many large companies and its cutting edge research to improve its communication system are key to keeping it strong.

Weibo (NASDAQ: WB)

Price at time of writing: $70.40 USD

Founded in 2008 and currently residing in San Francisco, CA, Weibo is a provider of web-based communication to businesses and allows the use of its APIs to enable a variety of communications like texts/calls via their databases.

Current sales stand at $650 million per year and climbing as the premier provider of these services to major companies and government entities.

It maintains low risk with very little competition in the area and is poised for a bright future in the industry. Its strong relationship with many large companies and its cutting edge research to improve its communication system are key to keeping it strong.

It is a good investment for anyone not scared of investment in China.

China Mobile (NASDAQ: CHL)

Price at time of writing: $47.14 USD

Founded in 1997 and currently residing in Hong Kong, China Mobile is a provider of wireless communications and wireless products. It is semi owned by the Chinese Government and enjoys a great deal of protections that others do not have.

Current sales stand at $16 billion per year and climbing as the premier provider of these services to major companies and government entities.

It maintains low risk with very little competition in the area and with the protection of the Chinese government, it is quickly expanding into rural areas of the country with unprecedented ability to cut consumer costs. Its strong relationship with many large companies and its cutting edge research to improve its communication system are key to keeping it strong.

It is a good investment for those not worried about potential fluctuations in the Chinese market.

Aurora Cannabis (NASDAQ: ACB)

Price at time of writing: $9.14 USD

Founded in 2013 and currently residing in Edmonton AB, Canada, Aurora Cannabis is a provider of marijuana and related products.

Current sales stand at $18 million per year and climbing as a premier provider of these services to all areas where marijuana is legal (and probably some that are not).

It maintains low risk with very little competition in the area and is poised for a bright future in the industry.

It is a good investment for anyone not scared of investment in cannabis or foreign businesses.

Aphria (NASDAQ: APHA)

Price at time of writing: $7.87 USD

Founded in 2014 and currently residing in Toronto, Canada, Aphria is a provider of marijuana and related products, mostly to the medical industry.

Current sales stand at $36 million per year and climbing as a premier provider of these services to all areas in the medical arena, which provides a much bigger market than some of its competitors that rely on the recreational market alone.

It maintains low risk with very little competition in the area and is poised for a bright future in the industry.

It is a good investment for anyone not scared of investment in cannabis or foreign businesses.

Tilray (NASDAQ: TLRY)

Price at time of writing: $51.24 USD

Founded in 2014 and currently residing in Narimo BC, Canada, Tilray is a provider of marijuana and related products.

Current sales stand at $30 million per year and climbing as a premier provider of these services, with distribution and branches in Germany, South America, Australia, and New Zealand. This provides a much bigger market than some of its competitors that rely on the North American market.

It maintains low risk with very little competition in the area and is poised for a bright future in the industry.

It is a good investment for anyone not scared of investment in cannabis or foreign businesses.

Intel (NASDAQ: INTC)

Price at time of writing: $58.82 USD

Founded in 1968 and currently residing in Santa Clara, CA, Intel is the number two (2nd only to Samsung) provider of semiconductors and wireless communications infrastructure and product components.

Current sales stand at $70 billion per year and climbing as a major provider of these services to large companies and government entities.

It maintains low risk with very little competition in the area and is poised for a bright future in the industry. Its strong relationship with many large companies and its cutting edge research to improve its communication system are key to keeping it strong.

It is a great investment for any investor!

Corning (NASDAQ: GLW)

Price at time of writing: $34.46 USD

Founded in 1852 and currently residing in Corning, NY, Corning is a provider of glass, ceramic, and wireless optics.

Current sales stand at $11 billion per year and climbing as the premier provider of these services to major companies and government entities.

It maintains low risk with very little competition in the area and is poised for a bright future in the industry. Its strong relationship with many large companies and its cutting edge research to improve its communication system are key to keeping it strong.

It is a great investment for any investor.

Comcast (NASDAQ: CMCSA)

Price at time of writing: $41.88 USD

Founded in 1953 and currently residing in Philadelphia, PA, Comcast is a provider of broadcasting, telecommunications, and streaming technologies. It is the result of a merger of several companies including NBC, Comcast, and a division of Verizon. Some of its holdings are cable powerhouses such as Syfy and Bravo, as well as the streaming giant HULU.

Current sales stand at $94 billion per year and climbing as the premier provider of these services to major companies and government entities. Its revenue has grown year after year, as shown in the recent sales chart on their website.

It maintains low risk with very little competition in the area and is poised for a bright future in the industry. Its strong relationship with many large companies and its cutting edge research to improve its communication system are key to keeping it strong.

Dell (NASDAQ: DELL)

Price at time of writing: $66.02 USD

Founded in 1984 and currently residing in Round Rock, TX, Dell is a provider of computers, parts, and wireless devices. It has made a name for itself with new innovations in logistics and supply chain operation.

Current sales stand at $78 billion per year and climbing as a premier provider of these products to individuals, major companies, and government entities.

It maintains average risk with the competition in the area and is poised for a bright future in the industry. Its strong relationship with many large companies, brand loyalty, and its cutting edge research to improve its products are a huge pro.

Chapter Seven Growth Stocks Part 4

Cloudera (NASDAQ: CLDR)

Price at time of writing: $10.91 USD

Founded in 2002 and currently residing in Palo Alto, CA, Cloudera is a provider of a software platform for data engineering, data warehousing, machine learning and analytics that runs in the cloud or on premises. Basically, it is a cloud computing repository provider.

Current sales stand at $650 million per year and climbing as a premier provider of these services to major companies and government entities.

It maintains low risk with very little competition in the area and is poised for a bright future in the industry. Its strong relationship with many large companies and its cutting edge research to improve its infrastructure are key to keeping it strong.

It is a strong investment for any investor of any level.

Equinix (NASDAQ: EQIX)

Price at time of writing: $452.50 USD

Founded in 1998 and currently residing in Redwood, CA, Equinix is a provider of internet connection and data centers.

Current sales stand at $4.5 billion per year and climbing as a rising provider of these services to major companies and government entities.

It is average to low risk with some competition in the area and is poised for a bright future in the industry. Its strong relationship with many large companies and its cutting edge research to improve its infrastructure are key to keeping it strong.

It is a very strong stock for those that can afford the purchase price.

FireEye (NASDAQ: FEYE)

Price at time of writing: $15.83 USD

Founded in 2004 and currently residing in Mittapis, CA, FireEye is a provider of cybersecurity and antivirus protection systems.

Current sales stand at $880 million per year and climbing as the premier provider of these services to major companies and government entities.

It maintains low risk with very little competition in the area and is poised for a bright future in the industry. Its strong relationship with many large companies and its cutting edge research to improve its communication system are key to keeping it strong.

It is a very strong stock for any investor at a very affordable price.

Intuit (NASDAQ: INTU)

Price at time of writing: $264.87 USD

Founded in 1983 and currently residing in Mountain View, CA, Intuit is a provider of web-based accounting, tax preparation, and bookkeeping under the brands TurboTax, Quickbooks, Mintm, and Proconnect.

Current sales stand at $5 billion per year and climbing as the premier provider of these services to individuals, major companies, and government entities. Its recent history of income was published on its website and shows consistent growth over time.

It maintains low risk with very little competition in the area and is poised for a bright future in the industry. Its strong relationship with many large companies and its cutting edge research to improve its delivery and pricing are key to keeping it strong.

Veeva Systems (NASDAQ: VEEV)

Price at time of writing: $137.37 USD

Founded in 2007 and currently residing in Pleasanton, CA, Veeva Systems is a provider of cloud-based and content management services.

Current sales stand at $65 billion per year and climbing as the premier provider of these services to major companies and government entities.

It maintains low risk despite competition in the area and is poised for a bright future in the industry. Its strong relationship with many large companies and its cutting edge research to improve its platforms are key to keeping it strong.

It is a strong stock for any investor.

Trade Desk (NASDAQ: TTD)

Price at time of writing: $208.27 USD

Founded in 2009 and currently residing in Ventura, CA, Trade Desk is a provider of web-based investing and brokerage services. It is one of the leaders in the direct investment sector that allows for instant purchases across several exchanges.

Current sales stand at $477 million per year and climbing as the premier provider of these services worldwide. Its recent financials as published on their investor relations page have shown excellent growth, indicating a strong position in the industry.

It maintains a low risk with very little new competition in the area and is poised for a bright future in the industry. Its strong relationships with the exchanges/customers and its cutting edge research to improve its communication system are key to keeping it strong.

Altogether this makes it a great stock for any investor.

Iron Mountain (NASDAQ: IRM)

Price at time of writing: $35.84 USD

Founded in 1951 and currently residing in Boston, MA, Iron Mountain is a provider of web-based and software-based enterprise information and data management.

Current sales stand at $3.5 billion per year and climbing as the premier provider of these services to major companies and government entities.

It maintains low risk with very little competition in the area and is poised for a bright future in the industry. Its strong relationship with many large companies and its cutting edge research to improve its communication system are key to keeping it strong.

It is a good stock for any level of investor.

IBM (NASDAQ: IBM)

Price at time of writing: $140.05 USD

Founded in 1911 and currently residing in Armont, NY, IBM initially started as a provider of office machines and later computers. Today it provides a plethora of computers, software, components, and wireless products to businesses, government, and individuals. It makes up one of the core companies of the DOW Jones Average.

Current sales stand at $79 billion per year and climbing as the premier provider of these services to major companies and government entities. IBM has battled back from recession losses to be sitting as a stable stock. The published earnings report on the IBM website shows excellent stability and growth in recent years.

It maintains low risk despite the competition in the area and is poised for a bright future in the industry. Its strong relationship with many large companies and its cutting edge research to improve its communication system are key to keeping it strong.

A very stable stock for any level of investor.

Taiwan Semiconductor (NASDAQ: TSM)

Price at time of writing: $45.41 USD

Founded in 1987 and currently residing in Taiwan, Taiwan Semiconductor is a provider of semiconductors and wireless infrastructure components.

Current sales stand at $15 billion per year and climbing as an on the rise provider of these products to major companies and government entities.

It maintains low risk despite the competition in the area and is poised for a bright future in the industry especially in the emerging Far East market. Its strong relationship with many large companies and its cutting edge research to improve its products will keep it strong.

A good investment for any investor not afraid of the emerging world.

Thermo Fisher Scientific (NASDAQ: TMO)

Price at time of writing: $263.95 USD

Founded in 2006 and currently residing in San Francisco, CA, Thermo Fisher Scientific resulted from a merger of Thermo Electron and Fisher Scientific. It is a provider of genetic research and micro-precision lab and medical equipment. It owns and supplies under many different brands including Thermo Scientific, Applied Biosystems, and Invitrogen.

Current sales stand at $20 billion per year and climbing as the premier provider of these services to major companies and government entities.

It maintains low risk with very little competition in the area and is poised for a bright future in the industry. Its strong relationship with many large companies and its cutting edge research to improve its systems are key to keeping it strong.

A wise investment for any level of investor.

Exact Sciences (NASDAQ: EXAS)

Price at time of writing: $95.46 USD

Founded in 1995 and currently residing in Madison, WI, Exact Sciences is a lab that concentrates on genetic and microbial research for the purpose of mapping risk down to the atom. It has an exclusive relationship with FDA and conducts a lot of trials for them.

Current sales stand at $6 billion per year and climbing as the premier provider of these services to major companies and government entities.

It maintains low risk with very little competition in the area and is poised for a bright future in the industry. Its strong relationship with many large companies and its cutting edge research to improve its communication system are key to keeping it strong.

A very economical and wise choice for any investor.

Myriad Genetics (NASDAQ: MYGN)

Price at time of writing: $32.24 USD

Founded in 1991 and currently residing in Salt Lake City, UT, Myriad Genetics is a provider of multiple types of genetic testing and other diagnostic products based on molecular biology. Its flagship product is Prolaris, which can map the risk of colon cancer and has extended the lives of many patients.

Current sales stand at $26 billion per year and climbing as the premier provider of these services to major companies and government entities.

It maintains low risk with very little competition in the area and is poised for a bright future in the industry. Its strong relationship with many large companies and its cutting edge research to improve its communication system are key to keeping it strong.

A very economical and wise choice for any investor.

NeoGenomics (NASDAQ: NEO)

Price at time of writing: $19.88 USD

Founded in 2002 and currently residing in Fort Myers, FL, NeoGenomics is a lab that concentrates on genetic and microbial research for the purpose of treating cancer.

Current sales stand at $10 billion per year and climbing as the premier provider of these services to major companies and government entities.

It maintains low risk with very little competition in the area and is poised for a bright future in the industry. Its strong relationship with many large companies and its cutting edge research to improve its communication system are key to keeping it strong.

A very economical and wise choice for any investor.

Nvidia (NASDAQ: NVDA)

Price at time of writing: $191.88 USD

Founded in 1992 and currently residing in Santa Clara, CA, Nvidia is a provider of platforms for gaming, data centers, auto, pro visualization, and now AI. It has garnered a following for its gaming CPUs. Per its website, it does business with the brands GeForce, Quadro, Tegra, and Tesla.

Current sales stand at $9 billion per year and climbing as the premier provider of these services to major companies and government entities.

It maintains low risk with very little competition in the area and is poised for a bright future in the industry. Its strong relationship with many large companies and its cutting edge research to improve its products are key to keeping it strong.

It is a very wise stock for any level of investor.

Micron Technology (NASDAQ: MU)

Price at time of writing: $43.20 USD

Founded in 1978 and currently residing in Boise, ID, Micron Technology is holding and parent company to many subsidiaries that produce computers and semiconductors, and wireless products.

Current sales stand at $20 billion per year and climbing as the premier provider of these services to major companies and government entities.

It maintains low risk with very little competition in the area and is poised for a bright future in the industry. Its strong relationship with many large companies and its cutting edge research to improve its technology system are key to keeping it strong.

Ross (NASDAQ: ROST)

Price at time of writing: $98.65 USD

Founded in 1982 and currently residing in Dublin, CA, Ross is a provider of name brand clothing for men, women, and children and consumer products in a secondary setting. It buys closeouts and overstocks and resells them at over 1000 stores across the Midwest and Northeast.

Current sales stand at $12 billion per year and climbing as the premier provider of these products at low prices. This type of store remains stable in a recession as discounting is big.

It maintains low risk with very little competition in the area and is poised for a bright future in the industry. Its great relationship with retailers and brand awareness is keeping it strong.

A recession proof stock which should hold strong in the coming 36 months.

Amgen (NASDAQ: AMGN)

Price at time of writing: $179.20 USD

Founded in 1980 and currently residing in Thousand Oaks, CA, Amgen works in the pharma industry related to preventing infection in chemotherapy patients and blocking betta transmitters in cancer cells.

Current sales stand at $23 billion per year and climbing as the premier provider of these services to medical providers and researchers.

It maintains low risk with very little competition in the area and is poised for a bright future in the industry. Its strong relationship with many large companies and its cutting edge research to improve its products is key to keeping it strong.

A high potential stock for any investor level.

Dollar Tree (NASDAQ: DLTR)

Price at time of writing: $109.85 USD

Founded in 1986 and currently residing in Norfolk, VA, Dollar Tree is a retailer of low-cost items, food, and consumer products under the Names Dollar Tree and Family Dollar across North America.

Current sales stand at $22 billion per year and climbing as the premier provider of discount items.

It maintains low risk with very little competition in the area and is poised for a bright future in the industry. Its strong relationship with many large companies and its cutting its many locations make it a primary stock and poised for success.

Like Ross, a good solid recession-proof stock for any investor.

Concho Resources (NASDAQ: CXO)

Price at time of writing: $128.31 USD

Founded in 2004 and currently residing in Midland, TX, Concho Resources is a provider of research into bio-carbon and alternative energies. Its vast petroleum holdings make it very successful.

Current sales stand at $4 billion per year and climbing as the premier provider of these services to major companies and government entities.

It maintains low risk with very little competition in the area and is poised for a bright future in the industry. Its strong relationship with many large companies and its cutting edge research to improve its energy offerings/green energy in general are key to keeping it strong.

Great for any investor, especially those interested in green energy.

Nutanix (NASDAQ: NTNX)

Price at time of writing: $43.02 USD

Founded in 2009 and currently residing in India, Nutanix is a provider of web-based cloud business solutions for hyper-converged infrastructure (HCI) appliances and software-defined storage.

Current sales stand at $700 million per year and climbing as the premier provider of these services to major companies and government entities in the Far and Middle East.

It maintains low risk with very little competition in the area and is poised for a bright future in the industry. Its strong relationship with many large companies and its cutting edge research to improve its communication system are key to keeping it strong.

A good investment for those not afraid of investing in the Middle East.

Dropbox (NASDAQ: DBX)

Price at time of writing: $23.42 USD

Founded in 2007 and currently residing in San Francisco, CA, Dropbox is a provider of online file sharing platforms in 17 languages that allow syncing and easy sharing of projects with people all over the world. It offers several levels of service each with different abilities and functions.

Current sales stand at $20 billion per year and climbing as the premier provider of these services to individuals, colleges/schools major companies and government entities.

It maintains low risk with very little competition in the area and is poised for a bright future in the industry. Its strong relationship with many large companies and its cutting edge research to improve its communication system are key to keeping it strong.

Competition from Google will be tough, but the market is big enough for both to co-exist.

Boingo Wireless (NASDAQ: WIFI)

Price at time of writing: $23.68 USD

Founded in 2001 and currently residing in Los Angeles, CA, Boingo Wireless is a provider of wireless internet service to enabled devices with over 1,000,000 wireless networks to use. It is an alternative to the major carriers and data services. It operates and sells a variety of products/services such as traditional wireless and broadband.

Current sales stand at $250 million per year and climbing as the premier provider of these services to major companies and government entities. Including various airports and transportation hubs.

It maintains low risk with very little competition in the area and is poised for a bright future in the industry. Its strong relationship with many large companies and its cutting edge research to improve its communication system are key to keeping it strong.

Genius Brands International (NASDAQ: GNUS)

Price at time of writing: $2.00 USD

Founded in 2013 and currently residing in Los Angeles, CA, Genius Brands International is an entertainment and animation company (formerly DIC) that formed as the result of multiple mergers. It is rebuilding its business and venturing into CGI. This is definitely a company to watch for the future.

Current sales stand at $300 million per year and climbing as it will be a premiere animation company going forward.

It maintains low risk despite the competition in the area due to its strong branding and its past favorites such as Inspector Gadget and Dennis the Menace.

With a industry-wide trend towards tried and true franchises, Genius Brands is poised to be on the up and up over the next few years.

Eastman Kodak (NASDAQ: KODK)

Price at time of writing: $2.46 USD

Founded in 1888 and currently residing in Rochester, NY, Eastman Kodak is a provider of various graphics and art products, software, and devices. It was once the leader in film and photography and invented the digital camera. It has struggled to make a comeback but is poised to reenter the market with its new medical imaging products as well.

It maintains low risk despite the competition in the area and is poised for a bright future in the industry. Its strong relationship with many large companies and its cutting edge research to improve its products, as well as its brand recognition are key to keeping it strong.

This one could go either way, but the medical imaging market potential makes it a solid play for any investor that is willing to buy and hold for an extended time.

Arcimoto (NASDAQ: FUV)

Price at time of writing: $4.00 USD

Founded in 2007 and currently residing in Eugene, OR, Arcimoto is a provider of electric motorized transportation, including tandem two and three wheel bikes. Poised in an industry that is erupting as people move away from cars, Arcimoto is poised to be a leader.

Current sales stand at $650 million per year and climbing as the premier provider of these products to the public.

It maintains low risk with very little competition in the area and is poised for a bright future in the industry. As the industry of green transportation grows so will it.

A great and cheap option for those willing to buy and hold for many years.

Conclusion

Investing your money in the stock market (or anywhere else!) can be overwhelming, but it doesn't have to be.

I hope this information has been beneficial to you and has given you a foundation to invest some of the more unknown companies. There has never been a more exciting time for the market than right now. Even if you feel like you missed the boat with the Apples and Amazons of the world, don't worry, it's never too to get your piece of the pie.

Using dollar cost averaging and putting money into the market each month is a great way to invest. It helps make your investing automatic and allows you to smooth out your investments into a market that moves up and down in an unpredictable way. Remember to do additional research outside of what you've learned in this book. And for your own sanity, don't check your investments on a daily basis. Growth stocks in particular can be a volatile market, and you have to be willing to accept that if you are to make long term profits. Perhaps most importantly, don't panic sell if you see a dip in the market. I wish you the best of luck in the cryptocurrency market, and I hope you make a lot of money.

www.ingramcontent.com/pod-product-compliance
Lightning Source LLC
Chambersburg PA
CBHW081815200326
41597CB00023B/4256